PUB WALKS
ON
MERSEYSIDE

Abigail Bristow and Norman James

Published by Sigma Leisure – an imprint of
Sigma Press, 1 South Oak Lane, Wilmslow, Cheshire SK9 6AR, England.

British Library Cataloguing in Publication Data
A CIP record for this book is available from the British Library.

ISBN: 1-85058-360-9

Typesetting and Design by: Sigma Press, Wilmslow, Cheshire.

Cover picture: The Boat House, Parkgate

Printed by: Manchester Free Press

Preface

"Pub Walks on Merseyside" contains descriptions of 150 miles of varied walks, ranging from dune and seaside strolls, to countryside rambles, to (very) gentle hillwalking and including some interesting and important town trails.

Merseyside as a county is a recent creation, carved out of Lancashire and Cheshire, yet the authors firmly believe that the area is sufficiently distinct to merit its separate identity. They hope that this book will allow visitors to Merseyside to appreciate the unique nature of Merseyside and its constituent towns and cities.

For such a small county with tightly drawn boundaries Merseyside enjoys a healthy diversity of geographical terrains. This book aims to reflect the multifarious walking terrains to be found in different parts of the county. Most of the walks are easy to moderate, reflecting the gentle nature of the Merseyside countryside. The authors make no apologies for including a number of town trails, which they consider to be indispensable in order to present a comprehensive picture of the nature of Merseyside.

"Pub Walks on Merseyside" invites you to experience Merseyside in all its aspects, and to sample many of its fine public houses. Each walk features at least one hostelry, and the text contains references to others where appropriate. Each of the pubs featured serves real ale, which the authors consider to be a most important companion to a good walk.

All the walks are accessible on a regular basis by public transport – Merseyside enjoys a very high quality bus and rail network – and details are given at the beginning of each walk. Access details by car are also given. Most of the pubs have their own car park where you may be able to park – provided, of course, that you intend to visit the pub on your return. Always let the landlord know what you are doing before setting out on the walk, in order to avoid any misunderstandings.

Finally, the authors hope that you obtain as much enjoyment from these walks as they did, and that you, too, experience the pleasure of sampling the real ale and unique atmosphere to be found in the pubs featured within this book.

Abigail Bristow

Norman James

CONTENTS

WIRRAL AND WEST CHESHIRE

Location Map (numbers refer to walks in this book)

AN INTRODUCTION TO MERSEYSIDE

From the windswept dykes of the Ribble Estuary, past the dunes and golf links of the Sefton coastline, through the heart of Liverpool with its port and Albert Dock complex, through the Knowsley Safari Park, along the canal in St Helens, across the Mersey by ferry or through the road tunnels, to the seaside resorts and country pursuits of Wirral . . . Merseyside is a diverse and attractive county of almost one and a half million inhabitants, despite being very compact with tightly-drawn boundaries. There are strong links to the neighbouring counties and districts: from Sefton to the West Lancashire plain and from Wirral to the Cheshire plain.

Merseyside is rightly world-famous for several reasons: its former economic prosperity largely founded upon the slave trade, the Beatles, Liverpool and Everton football clubs, the Albert Dock Complex, the Mersey Ferries, the Mersey Tunnels and, indeed, the people of Liverpool and Merseyside itself: outgoing, witty, sharp. Merseyside, despite its relative decline in recent years, is still a major industrial player, and offers a wide range of cultural and diverse entertainments.

Merseyside lies in the heart of England's North West. With its five districts of Liverpool, Knowsley, St Helens, Sefton and Wirral it provides a kaleidoscope of contrasts and opportunities which are difficult to match. Merseyside provides the ideal location for a day trip to take in one of its many attractions, as well as one of the fine pub walks in this publication; or alternatively, as the base for an exploration of the whole Merseyside area, again using the selection of the walks in this book which provides a good geographical mix of Merseyside locations.

Liverpool gained its town charter in 1207, and rapidly became the greatest British west coast port, shipping cotton and other manufactured goods around the world, dealing most notoriously in hundreds of thousands of slaves from West Africa, which laid the foundations for Liverpool's economic prosperity. The Mersey Maritime Museum gives an excellent insight into the history of Liverpool's marriage with the sea including the slave trade, and is well worth a visit in the Albert Dock. Liverpool was also the last English foothold for many emigrants who departed these shores to start a new life in the New World.

Geography

The north of Merseyside, Sefton, snaking along the coastline, is the Western edge of the West Lancashire Plain: geological and geographical ties join Sefton and Lancashire, while economic and social ties bind Sefton with Liverpool and the rest of Merseyside.

The coastal countryside of Sefton, rarely rising more than a few metres above sea level, offers a fascinating blend of sandy beaches, dunes and golf links. If you enjoy miles of golden sandy beaches, Sefton is the place for you! If you enjoy wandering the quiet and mysterious shifting dunes examining the attractive and rare flora and fauna within its many nature reserves, Sefton is also the place for you! And if you enjoy golf, and especially dunes links, including the world-famous Royal Birkdale Golf Club, Sefton is the place for you!

Liverpool is variously connected to the east of the country by rail (the Regional Railways Trans-Pennine Service) and by road (the M62); the Leeds-Liverpool Canal joins these two major towns winding through the Wigan coalfields. The canal is sadly not navigable, but a towpath exists along the length of the route for leisure enthusiasts. Manchester, Liverpool's great Lancastrian rival in so many spheres, lies just under an hour away by car or by train. These two great city rivals have vied through the centuries for Lancastrian supremacy. The Manchester Ship Canal takes over where the Mersey loses navigability, and adds a further transport connection. Speke Airport, to the south-east of Liverpool, provides daily connections to Ireland and the Isle of Man. It is currently overshadowed by its great North-Western rival: Manchester Airport.

The Royal Liver Building

St Helens and Knowsley occupy the flatlands between Liverpool and Wigan and Greater Manchester. The industrial revolution, and especially coal, were important here: sadly, Parkside Colliery in St Helens has just been closed by British Coal: the last pit in Merseyside. Pilkington Glass of St Helens is famous throughout the world, and provides a valuable source of employment.

Pass through the Mersey Tunnels and you come to Birkenhead and Wirral. Birkenhead, Liverpool's sister city, is a fine Victorian town. Much of the rest of Wirral relies on its coastal setting and attractive internal countryside. Wirral lies at the end of the Cheshire Plain, resting on deposits of red Cheshire sandstone which provides the building material for many of the local buildings. The Mersey lies to the east, the Dee to the west: these estuaries have shaped much of the history of Wirral and its inhabitants. The Dee Estuary is now a wonderful resting area for many estuarial and wading birds. Trippers and tourists still flock to the seaside resorts such as New Brighton and Parkgate: ramblers, horse riders and country lovers enjoy the interior of the Wirral for its footpaths, trails and nature reserves.

Liverpool

Liverpool is the largest of the five districts of Merseyside and sits at the heart of the conurbation. It lies on the River Mersey and its docks, now sadly shrunken in size, formerly stretched several miles to the north and to the south of the city centre, and were considered by some to be one of the modern wonders of the world. The extensive docks provided both the economic strength of Liverpool, and ultimately its industrial and economic weakness. Development of the docks and the resulting period of rapid industrialisation led to a dramatic increase in the size of Liverpool: from a population of 7,000 in 1708, to 77,000 in 1801, and to 223,000 in 1841.

Liverpool was the premier port in Britain, accounting for over 50 percent of the country's exports in certain products. The transport infrastructure linking Liverpool and the rest of the country was unrivalled: the Leeds-Liverpool Canal, the Weaver Navigation, the Bridgewater Canal, the Sankey Valley, St Helens Canal, the Manchester Ship Canal. These all contributed to the "golden triangle" of Liverpool's commercial wealth:

manufactured products from Britain to West Africa; slaves from West Africa to the West Indies and North America; and tobacco, sugar, rum and many other products from North America and the West Indies back to Britain.

Originally manufacturing industry was attracted to Liverpool by the commercial success generated by its docking activities. It was eventually decided that commerce and manufacture do not mix – all available labour in Liverpool was directed to docking activities, and in the main these labourers were unskilled – and manufacturing industry moved elsewhere, for example shipbuilding moved across the Mersey to Birkenhead, salt-processing (the forerunner of a major chemical industry) moved east along the Mersey to Widnes. When the port's activity contracted through a fall-off in traditional trading and the increased competition of other ports, Liverpool had no large-scale manufacturing base to fall back upon, and went into an unfortunate economic decline which to this day it is making strenuous efforts to overcome.

Knowsley

Knowsley is the administrative district to the east of Liverpool, centred upon Huyton, once the parliamentary constituency of the former Prime Minister, Harold Wilson. So proud of him were the people of Huyton that a public house has been named in honour of him – "The Pipe and Gannex" – these were the trademarks of the Wilson premiership. Knowsley is famous these days as the site of the Knowsley Safari Park, which is very popular with trippers and Merseyside residents alike.

Sefton

Sefton hugs the coastline north of Liverpool as far as the Ribble Estuary. Its two major towns are Bootle to the south, with its still important docks, and Southport to the north, a fine and genteel Victorian watering place with many grand streets and ornate shopping arcades. Between these two towns lie the miles of dunes which give Sefton its unique characteristic: these dunelands almost seem to be a different planet. Walk among these dunes and enjoy the unique flora and fauna which they spawn. Sefton forms the coastal strip of the West Lancashire Plain.

St Helens

St Helens was founded on the coal-mining industry: it produced the coal which fired the industry which produced the manufactures to provide the British exporting end of the commercial maritime triangle based upon the Liverpool docks. The last colliery in Merseyside, Parkside, sadly closed in 1993. The major industry in town is now provided by Pilkington Glass, famous the world over for its glass products. Carr Mill Dam is a pleasant leisure facility, and St Helens rugby league team is one of the greats in the game. St Helens is a fiercely proud and parochial place: Liverpudlians are considered foreigners here, but a warm welcome awaits the tripper or tourist who comes to explore a little of the area.

Wirral

Wirral lies across the Mersey from Liverpool, connected to its big brother by the Mersey road and rail Tunnels. The world-famous Mersey Ferries provide the surface cross-estuarial link. Birkenhead, with its magnificent Victorian centre-piece – Hamilton Square – forms the major conurbation on Wirral. Its strength rested on shipbuilding: again, sadly, the last shipbuilders closed in 1993. New Brighton is a fine and under-rated seaside resort, as is West Kirby. The interior of Wirral provides many miles of pleasant country walks, and from the summit of Thurstaston Hill the whole of the Northern end of the Wirral Peninsula is laid out before you. Lord Leverhulme chose Wirral as the site for his unique work of industrial philanthropy and paternalism: the workers' village at Port Sunlight.

Wirral possesses a wealth of natural, architectural and historic interest: for example, the bird sanctuaries of the Dee Estuary and the off-shore islands of Hilbre; Bidston Hill and heathland; and Royden Park and Thurstaston Common. Wirral is truly a magnificent setting for lively towns, tranquil villages, rural areas and, of course, excellent public houses.

SOME MERSEYSIDE THEMES

The Slave Trade

By the last decade of the 18th century, Liverpool was the leading slave-trading port of Great Britain. It had achieved this position in just fifty years, leaving London and Bristol trailing in its wake. This inglorious history is detailed well in the Mersey Maritime Museum. Basically, the Liverpool merchants managed to undercut their competitors in Bristol and London by paying lower wages to their skippers and other staff. Everyone was exploited in the slave trade.

The slave trade is naturally to be condemned, yet were those Liverpool merchants who ran it necessarily worse morally than merchants, traders and industrialists elsewhere, who relied on elements of the slave trade to further their commerce and moneymaking? Generally, it is fair to say that all Atlantic trade was linked closely with, and depended to a large extent upon, the slave trade: the carriage of sugar was cheaper because slaves were there to load it for England; everyone who worked in Lancashire or the Midlands, or anyone who smoked or took sugar in tea, was encouraging the slave trade and benefiting indirectly from it. Those who financed the slave ships and profited from the trade kept themselves detached from the sordid business: all they chose to see were the accounts and the goods imported from North America and the West Indies. It was the ships' crews – often little better than slaves themselves – and pressed into service when men were scarce, who had to cope with the true realities of the slave trade; this was a trade in human misery and greed. The slave trade was good capitalist business: the millions of lives lost or blighted by the slave trade were not to stand in the way of the pursuit of wealth.

Ports and Shipbuilding

The development of the Port of Liverpool and the over-dependence of the city on this maritime trade is detailed elsewhere in this introduction. Allied to the port activities was a substantial shipbuilding industry, firstly in Liverpool, and latterly in Birkenhead. Ships built on the Mersey sailed the world, and appeared under a bewildering variety of flags. The Mersey was truly one of the world's major maritime centres. The last shipbuilding yard in Birkenhead closed in 1993.

The Beatles

The four *"petits garçons de Liverpool"* heralded a new wave of popular music: did they institute the change, or were they fortunate to be taken forward on the crest of a musical new wave? You can find out about this, and all the other facts relating to John, Paul, George and Ringo, at the Beatles Museum within the Albert Dock complex. What is certain, though, is that these four musicians continued to carry the fame of Liverpool to the four corners of the earth. Liverpool was the music centre of the world, while The Beatles reigned.

Football

It is impossible to discuss Liverpool without mentioning its famous football teams: Liverpool and Everton. As the late Bill Shankly put it: "Football is not a matter of life and death; it's more important than that." The importance of football to the life of the city was most evident in the wake of the Hillsborough disaster when the whole city was genuinely in mourning. Liverpool were the dominant English side of the eighties, although Everton surpassed them (briefly) in the mid-eighties. Mention must also be made of the newly renascent Tranmere Rovers across the river in Wirral, and pressing to join their illustrious big city rivals in the Premier League.

Albert Dock

The Albert Dock complex, latterly restored to life after lying derelict for years, has now become one of the major tourist attractions in the country. It houses a range of shopping malls including fascinating shops, restaurants, cafes, bars and pubs; the Tate Gallery; the Beatles Museum; and the Mersey Maritime Museum with its unique blend of floating exhibits, working displays and craft demonstrations. Exhibitions focus on emigration, shipbuilding and other aspects of Liverpool's rich maritime heritage. The Albert Dock is open from 10.00 am daily.

Albert Dock

Tourist Information

For leaflets and information about places of interest and events throughout Merseyside, call in at the Merseyside Tourist Information Centres:

Merseyside Welcome Centre, Clayton Square, Liverpool L1 1QR; Tel: 051 709 3631

Tourist Information Centre, Albert Dock, Liverpool L3 4AA; Tel: 051 708 8854

These offices can also give advice on the Beatles Magical History Tour and the City Sightseeing Tour, as well as offering theatre and accommodation bookings, local transport and excursion tickets, and a wide range of souvenirs and guide books.

Sights worth seeing

The preceding paragraphs give some ideas for places to visit in Merseyside, and within the thirty walks in this book many other places of interest are featured. The authors have compiled the following list of personal preferences, which does not claim to be exhaustive. Telephone for details of opening hours:

❑ Anglican Cathedral: 051 709 6271

❑ Metropolitan Cathedral: 051 709 9222

❑ Liverpool Museum: 051 207 0001

❑ Walker Art Gallery: 051 207 0001

❑ Merseyside Maritime Museum: 051 207 0001

❑ Museum of Liverpool Life: 051 207 0001

❑ Pilkington Glass Museum: 0744 692499

❑ Birkenhead Priory: 051 666 1249

❑ Tate Gallery, Albert Dock: 051 709 3223

❑ Liverpool Town Hall: 051 236 5181

❑ Southport Botanic Gardens: 0704 27547

❑ Stadt Moers Park, Knowsley: 051 489 1239

❑ Sankey Valley Park, St Helens: 0744 39252

❑ Sefton Park, Liverpool

❑ Otterspool Promenade, Liverpool

❑ The Beatles Story, Albert Dock: 051 709 1963

❑ Mersey Ferries: 051 639 0609

❑ Knowsley Safari Park: 051 430 9009

❑ Southport Pleasureland and Zoo: 0704 532717

❑ Port Sunlight Heritage Centre: 051 644 6466

❑ Southport Pier: 0704 533500

❑ Speke Hall: 051 427 7231

THE WALKS

A major feature of Merseyside is the dominance of water: the county has a long coastline and includes the estuary of the Mersey. Merseyside is bounded to the south-west by the Dee estuary and to the north by the Ribble estuary. Man-made waterways are also a major feature reflecting the long industrial history of the area, notably the Leeds – Liverpool and St Helens canals. This means that many walks are possible along coastline or river banks – in the case of the Dee, ex-river banks where the water has retreated – and canal towpaths.

Our aim has been to construct interesting walks, each featuring at least one real ale pub along its route, spread throughout Merseyside. The walks include countryside, coastline, waterways and urban areas. We have ventured beyond the boundaries of Merseyside, to increase the scope and variety of the walks described, but only to those areas which have strong social, geographic or economic links to Merseyside. This is particularly necessary in the north of the County where the boundary is tightly drawn to include the coastal towns of Southport and Formby but excludes their rural hinterland. There are one or two walks which lie wholly outside Merseyside, but they are easily accessible, via local rail links.

Terrain

Notes on the walks and the maps provided clearly indicate the terrain. We use public footpaths and sections of two long distance paths: the Sefton Coastal Footpath and the Wirral Way. Merseyside is based around the conurbation of Liverpool, and we have included several town trails, which illustrate some of the essential features of the region. The amount of road walking involved is indicated; inevitably the town walks will be mainly road-based, but we have avoided the busiest roads.

Merseyside is blessed, perhaps surprisingly to an outsider, with a great amount of countryside, reflecting a variety of terrains and landscapes, for what is basically an urban county. We hope we have been able to express the full range of Merseyside's diversity in our selection of walks.

Access

The walks described in this book are based in and around Merseyside and vary in length from 2.5 to 9.5 miles. Most of the walks are circular, returning you to your starting point. The linear walks are – all but one – designed to take you from one railway station to another, so that a local train may be used to return you to your starting point. Local trains run to a very frequent timetable. The one exception involves the use of a local bus service.

Walk descriptions all include details of how to get to the start point by train or bus. The use of public transport instead of the car is better for the environment; it also avoids any disputes about who is going to drive and thus forgo the real ale treats offered by the pubs on the route. At present, local rail and bus links are excellent in most areas of Merseyside. We have not included timetable details as service timings are liable to change. We can only speculate as to the potential impact of rail privatisation. Telephone numbers to contact for current service information are given in the text of each walk.

Equipment

Merseyside offers a friendly walking environment; you are rarely far from human habitation, and the gradients are gentle. No special equipment is necessary for these walks save stout, comfortable shoes or boots. However, it is always wise to carry a light waterproof jacket and perhaps a spare jumper as the weather can be unpredictable and a soaking rarely enhances the pleasure of a walk. On longer walks a snack and something to drink may be usefully carried – walking in the sun can be very dehydrating and a bottle of water may be welcome.

The maps included show the route of the walk and should be adequate for you to find your way. However, the relevant Ordnance Survey Pathfinder Map is a useful backup.

Walking in the Countryside

Many of the walks take you across working countryside; it is as well to remember that the land you cross provides a farmer's livelihood. The rules for walking in the countryside are in the main based on common sense, however, it is worth mentioning a few of them. It is always important to keep to the line of the footpath, not to drop litter and, when you open a gate to pass through, always remember to shut and secure it behind you. If you are walking with a dog, please keep it on a lead when crossing farmland, and be especially careful in Spring during the lambing season when even the best behaved dog can cause problems. It is also important to remember not to pick flowers or other plants when out walking; many plants need to set seeds to reappear the following year, and left in place everyone can enjoy them. Sorry, if any of this sounds obvious, but it is necessary to treat the countryside with respect in order for everyone to enjoy it to the full.

Directions

We have endeavoured to make the directions given as clear as possible, especially where the route becomes a little complex. It is important to remember that the landscape changes over time, hedgerows are particularly vulnerable to grubbing up to increase field sizes.

THE PUBS

The pubs in this book share one feature, in that they all offer a good pint of real ale. We consider this as a crucial qualification – after all, a pub without good beer becomes a cafe, restaurant, wine bar or simply a poor pub. The defining feature of a pub must be its beer. The pubs are also pleasant in their atmosphere, and the lone walker will feel comfortable.

The pubs vary a great deal reflecting their location and role. One pub we visited, in a fairly isolated area, not only serves food on the premises but also acts as the local take-away. Others are old, new, original, refurbished, isolated, urban – in short they are all different.

Opening Times

The recent liberalisation of opening hours has brought about a great variety of timings, therefore we list the opening times with the pub entry. One piece of shorthand used is "normal Sunday opening hours" which in translation means that the pub is open on Sundays from 12 noon to 3 pm and again from 7 pm to 10.30 pm. Many pubs listed offer all day Sunday opening, but outside the "normal" hours the legal requirement is that alcohol may only be served with a meal.

The opening hours listed were provided to us by the publicans and are therefore as accurate as it is possible to make them. However, if you are planning a long walk, which depends for a happy conclusion on a certain pub being open at a specific time, it is always worth phoning to check that it will indeed be open.

The Beers

Pubs in Merseyside offer a wide range of beers, despite the recent brewery closures in Liverpool. However, the revival of Cains Brewery in Liverpool offers a bright spot on the horizon. Whitbread pubs are common in the area, and many now offer a selection of beers from the Whitbread cask collection.

In the Wirral and Cheshire local breweries whose beers may be found easily include Greenall Whitley of Warrington, Burtonwood from Burtonwood and Tetley, Walker of Warrington. A rarer product is that supplied by the Oak Brewery of Heywood, Greater Manchester and a newcomer is Weetwood.

If you are interested in searching out more pubs serving real ale in Merseyside, the local branches of CAMRA (the Campaign for Real Ale) have produced a guide "The Best Pubs Around Merseyside" which covers not only Merseyside but the hinterland areas of Cheshire, Lancashire and Deeside. A regular magazine "Mersey Drinker" is also produced giving up-to-the-minute information on beers and pubs. "Traditional Pubs of Old Lancashire", an independent publication from Sigma Leisure, also covers this area and emphasises pub architecture and interiors.

1. CROSSENS

Route: Crossens – Fiddlers Ferry – Banks Enclosed Marsh – Banks – Crossens

Distance: 9.5 miles

Map: OS Pathfinder 678 (1:25000) Blackpool (and Pathfinder 688 for a short stretch)

Start: The Plough at Crossens, located on roundabout with the A565 (SD375204)

Access: Accessible by bus from Southport; there is a bus stop on the roundabout. Contact Merseytravel on 051 236 7676 for bus service details. The A565 Preston to Southport coast road passes through the roundabout for car access, and there is limited on street parking.

Fleetwood House, Banks (0704 25018)

This is very much a two-bar pub. To the left is a lovely old basic local bar, where the only noise is that of enthusiastic dominoes players, and it is surprising how much noise dominoes can generate. The lounge to the right, accessible around the back of the bar or though a side entrance is plusher and has music, though oddly this is not audible in the other bar. Wherever you chose to sit, the Tetleys Mild and Bitter will be welcome.

The Fleetwood House is open all day Monday to Saturday, with normal opening hours on Sunday. Food is available at lunchtimes Monday to Saturday.

Banks

Banks is clearly an agricultural community, the houses often interspersed with market gardens and fields. The village is centred on the Fleetwood House pub and the beautiful church of St Stephen opposite.

The Walk

1. From The Plough take the third exit (i.e. opposite The Plough) on the right of the roundabout, Banks Road. The houses soon give way to fields and Crossens Pumping Station to the right.

2. After crossing the sluice, opposite the Pumping Station, turn left and cross a stile to the left of a metal gateway. Follow a wide path, fenced on both sides which bears left then right losing the fencing on the left in the process. The path becomes a raised ridge, with the river Ribble to the left. The path enters a National Nature Reserve, Ribble Estuary; one of the largest in England, which serves as an important bird sanctuary.

    The ridge straightens out and forms a break between the cultivated fields of Banks Enclosed Marsh to the right and the marshy estuary, forming grazing land and a bird haven to the left. Across the estuary Blackpool Tower can be seen on all but very hazy days, while the hills of Lancashire come into view ahead.

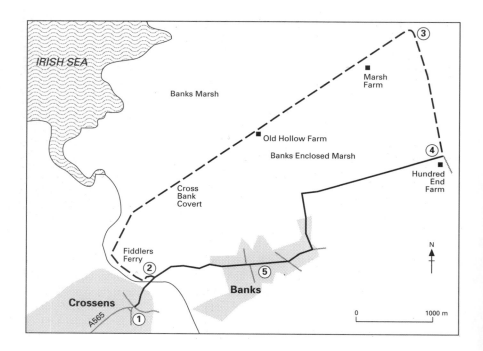

Cross a stile in a wooden fence across the ridge. Cross Bank Covert to the right breaks the line of the fields. Cross another stile, and the buildings of Cross Farm lie ahead. There is a path off to the right, but we stay on the ridge. A canalised ditch lies to the left of the ridge. From here Lytham St Annes is visible to your left across the estuary.

Walk on past a hide located on the ridge by the farm buildings, cross two stiles which take you over a road down to the marshes, to continue along the ridge.

A boat sits to the left of the ridge, either abandoned or in the early stages of renovation. At present, it just looks weird so far from the sea. Carry on along the ridge past Marsh Farm to your left and over a stile.

Boat at rest, Ribble Estuary

3. At the next stile, the ridge divides with one arm following the previous line parallel to the sea, while the other turns away to the right heading inland. Cross the stile and follow the ridge that turns inland. There are fields to either side now, cabbages are a dominant feature. Dairy cows graze either

side of the ridge, between the fields. Butterflies are common in summer. As you near the road, trees appear on both sides of the ridge.

4. Follow the ridge right to the end, where a stile takes you onto the road, turn right past Hundred End Farm and Marcliff Kennels. The road curves through farmland, and gains a footpath after a few hundred yards. If you look to your right, Blackpool Tower is still visible. The road curves left and then right into the village of Banks. At first it runs through a mixture of fields and housing, as it curves right it changes its name to Chapel Lane. Even as the centre is approached, it is clearly an agricultural community. The road takes you past Banks Methodist church and School on the left, then bends right past the Village Stores and changes name again to Bonds lane. Around the next bend it becomes Church road. Carry on past a small Co-op, garage and Post Office.

5. At this point the Fleetwood House pub comes into view on the left-hand side of the road, opposite a church – time for a welcome break. On leaving the pub continue along Church Road, past the Parish church of St Stephen. The

Fleetwood House coat of arms

road again changes its name, this time to the intriguing "Ralph's Wife's Lane". Red brick villas from the closing years of the last century line the road, before farmland takes over. Once again, Blackpool Tower is visible to the right. Back into housing again, look out for the tiny black and white Wood Cottage to the left. Soon the pumping station comes back into view; continue back along Banks Road to The Plough at Crossens. You may wish to sample the beer and food served in the Plough: a pleasant pub which was serving beers from the Whitbread Cask Collection at the time of the authors' visit. There is also a children's play area.

2. SOUTHPORT

Route: Southport Railway Station – Southport Pier – Promenade – Hesketh Park – Churchtown – Botanic Gardens

Distance: 5 miles

Map: OS Pathfinder 698 (1:25000) Southport; a street plan of Southport, available from the Tourist Information Office is useful but not essential.

Start: Southport Railway Station (SD338172)

Access: A frequent rail service operates between Liverpool and Southport. Check with Merseytravel on 051 236 7676 for rail service details.

If arriving by car on the A565, parking space is available along the seafront.

Hesketh Arms, Churchtown (0704 27084)

The Hesketh Arms is an attractive pub by the church and village green. The outside tables are very attractive when the sun shines. Beers available at the time of our visit included Cains Bitter and Tetleys Bitter, both excellent. Food is available lunch and evenings Monday to Saturday, and at Sunday lunchtimes. The Hesketh Arms is open all day Monday to Saturday (11.00 am to 11.00 pm); normal Sunday opening hours apply.

The Hesketh Arms in its present form dates back to the 1790s; the original building probably dates from the 17th century, when it formed three fishermen's cottages. In 1988 it won the Best Steak and Kidney Pie in Britain competition.

Bold Arms Hotel, Churchtown (0704 28192)

The Bold Arms is also located on the village square area and serves a variety of real ales including beers from Tetley Walker, Jennings, Hartleys and Robinsons. The pub has been comfortably refurbished, with wood and stained glass used to good effect, the fireplaces are also impressive. There is a floor-length window with seats at the back of the pub. Tables are available outside. An interesting menu is served at lunchtime every day, complete with a children's menu. Families are welcomed, and a children's area is available. The Bold Arms is open all day Monday to Saturday, and at normal hours on Sundays. A beer festival is held every Summer in the pub featuring 30 different real ales.

The Bold Arms Hotel

Churchtown

Churchtown is a conservation area centred on the church of St Cuthbert. There is a remarkable abundance of thatched roofs. It is a very attractive, peaceful village though situated on the outskirts of Southport. The very pleasant Botanic Gardens are located here and are well worth a visit; they contain not just a variety of flowers, shrubs and trees but also a museum, lake and aviary.

The Walk

This walk is a linear one from Southport railway station to Churchtown. A bus ride back is recommended; at present, a frequent service operates between Churchtown and Southport, check with Merseytravel on 051 236 7676 for the latest timetable.

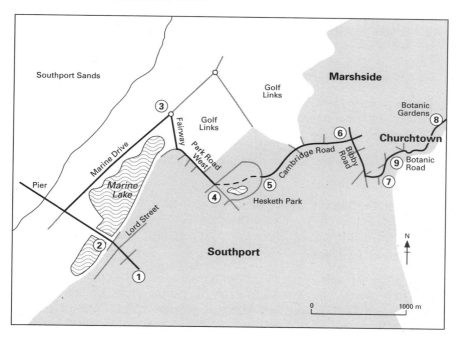

1. Exit Southport railway station to find yourself facing Woolworths, turn right along Chapel Street then immediately left down London Street. As you cross Lord Street, the impressive war memorial, erected by local subscription in 1923 to commemorate the dead of the Great War, dominates the view, the central obelisk is sixty feet high.

   Lord Street contains many interesting buildings and a town trail leaflet is available from the Tourist Information office. For this walk, cross Lord Street and continue down towards the Promenade.

2. The Pier is straight ahead, past a severe-looking statue of Queen Victoria. (If piers hold no attraction for you, turn right at the Pier entrance and then immediately left along Marine Parade, at the end of which you rejoin the walk by turning right onto Marine Drive.) The pier is well worth a visit: it is a remarkable survivor of a bygone era, and there is even a miniature railway running the length of the pier. You can ride the train for 70 pence (adult return fare) or walk the pier for an entrance fee of 30 pence (adult). When you reach the end of the pier, the sea is still likely to be far in the distance at low tide. Blackpool Tower is clearly visible to the right of the pier. To the left lies Pleasure Land, where Bungee jumpers may be seen swinging happily. A light aircraft takes advantage of the flat, firm, vast expanse of sand to offer flights around the coast.

   Return along the pier, but as the pier crosses the road, take the steps down to your left, cross the road and walk along the Promenade (Marine Drive) Northwards.

   The Marine Lake lies to your right, the sea to your left, somewhere beyond the sands.

3. About three quarters of a mile along the promenade turn right at the roundabout down Fairway – the Municipal Golf Links lie to your left. At the T-junction turn left along Park Road West, passing the 18th green, and a thirties-style club house.

4. At the junction with Albert Road lies an entrance to Hesketh Park. Follow the path around the lake full of seagulls, geese, ducks and ducklings (in spring). The park is large and attractive, with an aviary. Continue past the children's playground and a cafe to an exit marked by gateposts onto The Crescent.

5. Exit the park and turn left onto the Crescent. At the roundabout turn right down Cambridge Road (the A565 to Preston), a wide tree-lined road. If by chance you exit the Park at a different gate, follow round the Crescent until you come to Cambridge Road. Note "Cockle Dicks Lane" to the left. Walk on past the Parish Church of Emmanuel, which has a curious metal spire atop a red brick structure.

6. Turn right down Bibby Road, cross Beresford Road and continue down Bibby Road, there are some very attractive cottages on this junction, low lying black and white buildings. Take a left turn down Peets Lane.

7. At the end of Peets Lane turn left, past an attractive thatched cottage, into Botanic Road. A little way down Botanic Road you reach the attractive square, where lie the two pubs both well worth a visit.

8. Before or indeed after a visit to the pub, continue along Botanic Road, about 100 yards past the Hesketh Arms to find the Botanic Gardens, which are very interesting, do not miss the small fern house.

9. To return to Southport, retrace your steps back along Botanic Road until you reach a bus stop, about two hundred yards from the Bold Arms Hotel. The bus service is a frequent one at present, but it is probably worth checking the timetable before you set out, as bus services are prone to change frequently since the deregulation of bus services in 1986.

3. BESCAR

Route: Bescar – Scarisbrick – Pinfold – Heatons Bridge – Bescar

Distance: 6 miles

Map: OS Pathfinder 698 (1:25000) Southport

Start: The Swan Public House, Bescar Lane. (SD396146)

Access: Bescar lies north-west of Ormskirk off the A570, at Bescar Lane the only available parking is on-street. The Swan has a car park for patrons only.

Bescar Lane railway station is next to The Swan, frequencies vary. Telephone British Rail on 051 709 9696 for service details.

The Swan, Bescar Lane (0704 880238)

The Swan is a large welcoming pub with separate bar and lounge areas, there is also a large garden. The beers are from Tetleys and include the bitter and two milds: the dark mild was superb when the authors visited. Theakstons Bitter is also normally available. It is open all day Monday to Saturday, and at normal hours on Sunday. Look out for its happy hours. Food is available at lunchtimes every day. Families are welcomed, and there is an adventure playground.

The pub is sited very close to what used to be Britain's largest lake – The Mere – before it was drained to make way for farmland.

Heatons Bridge Inn, Heatons Bridge Road (0704 840549)

The Heatons Bridge Inn is a small cosy pub, with real fires. There are tables outside for warmer days. The beers are again from Tetleys and the mild was gorgeous. The pub is open all day Monday to Saturday, and at normal Sunday opening hours. Food is available every lunchtime except

Sunday. Children are welcomed, though currently only in the garden area. There are plans for a family dining room due to have been completed in 1993.

Bescar

Bescar is a small village, with an attractive 19th century Catholic church of St Elizabeth. Bescar is an agricultural community: the fields here-abouts are stuffed full with a variety of root vegetables.

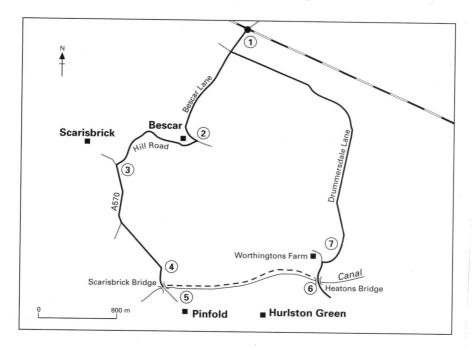

The Walk

1. From The Swan public house go left down the road away from the railway station. The walk takes you past the Methodist chapel on your right and continue down Bescar Lane. After about half a mile the attractive village of Bescar is reached, continue along the road until you arrive at a T-junction.

2. At this point, the Catholic church dating from 1888 is directly ahead of you. However, it is necessary to turn right at this T-junction along Hill Road. As the walk continues down this road, a strange old barn-like construction may be seen to your left across the fields. After about a mile a T-junction with traffic lights is reached.

3. Turn left at the traffic lights onto the main A570 signposted to Ormskirk and St Helens. If you are in need of a drink or a rest at this point, the Morris Dancers, a Beefeater Inn, is located on this junction. Otherwise carry on down the road, which takes you past Scarisbrick Hall School. Sadly, the Hall, a Victorian Gothic construction, is not visible from the road. It was occupied by the Scarisbrick family until 1948 and is now a private school. The grounds are private; however, on one day each year, the public are admitted. If you wish to time your walk to coincide with this rare opportunity, contact Lancashire County Council on Preston 54868 to discover the date.

4. As the walk continues down the road, a medieval weeping cross is to be seen to your left, just off the road in the grounds of Scarisbrick Hall. The road now rises to cross the canal; we turn right down a flight of steps onto the towpath just before the bridge.

5. Turn left and walk along the towpath of the Leeds – Liverpool Canal. The bridge here at Pinfold, was the spot where travellers from Liverpool alighted from the canal to continue their journey to Southport by coach. Immediately past the bridge, the remains of Wheelwrights Wharf may be seen on the opposite bank of the canal: the wharf was mainly used for the transit of night soil. Such is the steamy history of many canals!

   Stroll along the canal path, past moorings for many narrow boats. After about half a mile a bridge will be visible ahead.

6. Pass through a kissing gate, and then turn left up the steps onto the road. Turn right over Heatons Bridge, so named because the building of the Leeds – Liverpool Canal cut across the fields of Evan Heatons Farm, splitting it in two. The Heatons Bridge Inn is right next to the canal: time for a welcome pint of Tetleys.

   On leaving the pub turn left back across the bridge, and this time continue along Dam Wood Lane: very soon turn right onto Drummersdale Lane.

7. This Lane takes you through open farmland, mainly root vegetables, though

the odd free range hen or goose may be spotted. One of the farms to the left, Worthingtons Farm, was the site where, in 1665, Hugh Worthington ploughed up more than three hundred Roman silver coins. Continue along this lane and the outskirts of Bescar are soon reached. When you come to the cross roads by the corner store, turn right, following the direction for Bescar Lane Station. Soon you will be back at The Swan: time for a pint of Tetleys while you await your train.

The Swan at Bescar

4. AINSDALE

Route: Ainsdale Railway Station – Sefton Coastal Walk – Birkdale Railway Station

Distance: 4.5 miles

Map: OS Pathfinder 698 (1:25000) Southport

Start: Ainsdale Railway Station (SD311123)

Access: The station is served by a regular service between Liverpool and Southport: for service details contact Merseytravel on 051 236 7676.

For those arriving by car off the A565, there is a car park by the railway station.

Fisherman's Rest, Birkdale (0704 69986)

This is an unusual building, very attractive externally, recently renovated inside. The Fisherman's Rest is all that remains of the once renowned Palace Hotel, which was demolished in 1969 at the age of 103 years. The Fisherman's Rest is named after the role played by the Hotel in the aftermath of a famous shipping disaster in 1886. Two lifeboats were sunk with the loss of all hands while attempting to come to the rescue of the skipper and crew of the 92 ton Mexico bound for South America. The recovered bodies of the crew of the Eliza Fernley lifeboat were laid out on straw at the stables of the Palace Hotel, awaiting the coroner's inquest and formal identification. This is now the site of the Fisherman's Rest, and explains the pub's name. Ironically the whole crew of the Mexico was eventually rescued by a third lifeboat. The history behind the name is depicted on the walls of "The Fish".

Real ales available at the time of our visit included a rare treat in Youngers 70/-, also Youngers IPA and Theakstons XB. Generous bar meals are served at lunchtime Monday to Saturday, and children are welcomed when eating. There are some outside benches. The pub is open all day Monday to Saturday, and on Sundays observes the normal hours.

The Fisherman's Rest

Park Hotel, Birkdale (0704 69941)

The Park Hotel was built in the mid-nineteenth century as a hotel; its owner, James Marshbank, also ran a coal and guano business from the same site. Ownership passed to Matthew Brown in the mid 1920s, now part of the Scottish and Newcastle Estate. This is a quiet, comfortable pub with a reasonably priced menu, food being available between 11.30 am and 7.00 pm Monday to Saturday. Beers available include Matthew Brown Bitter and Theakstons XB, Marstons Pedigree and guest beers of the month. The Park Hotel is open 11.00 am to 11.00 pm Monday to Saturday, and at normal opening hours on Sunday. Children are welcomed, and there is an outdoor drinking area. This pub is very handy for Birkdale railway station.

Ainsdale & Birkdale

These two towns, now very much dormitory communities of the Merseyside heartland, are connected by links and dunes: golf courses line the coastline here including Royal Birkdale, the setting for many famous British Golf Open Championships. Ainsdale's name may mean "low-lying land", reflecting its topography. Birkdale means "beech tree valley", a name not necessarily rooted in historical accuracy.

The Walk

The walk is linear from Ainsdale railway station to Birkdale railway station, allowing you to return to Ainsdale by Merseyrail. Alternatively a return walk along the beach is attractive given the fine weather which is invariably experienced in this part of the world.

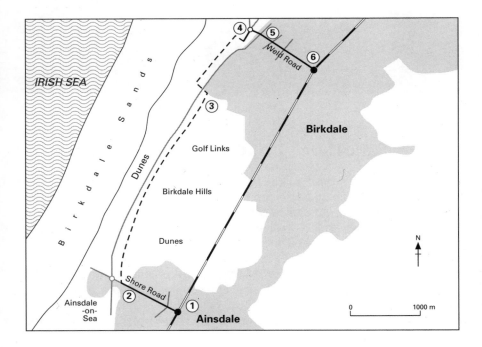

1. From the station car park turn left along Shore Road, continue along the road until it bends left, we go straight on along Shore Road down towards the sea.

2. The Birkdale Sandhills Local Nature Reserve is to the right, enter through the second gateway in the wooden fence. The reserve contains a variety of plant and wildlife, although on our visit we did not see the rarer residents; namely, the Natterjack toad and the Sand Lizard. Follow the white marker posts which eventually run parallel to the coast road. Continue along the path through the Dunes, past a sign telling you that Birkdale Railway Station lies three miles ahead. Small ponds lie to the right; each time the path forks, keep with the one closer to the road. However, if you wish to wander among the dunes it is possible to do so and then return to the path running alongside the road.

   After about a mile and half of dune walking, the first golfers become visible through the dunes to your right, giving a strange view of manicured dunes and grass on the golf course while you walk through the untamed rougher dunes. The path takes you away from the road for a short stretch.

3. If you prefer a level path, carry on along the path between the large houses at the end of the golf course and the road and re-join the main route at *point 5*. Otherwise, just before you reach the row of houses at the end of the golf course, a gap in the fence gives a clear point at which the road can be crossed. Cross the road here and walk straight up a sandy path into the dunes. The path soon bears right and the traffic noise fades as the dunes form a barrier between you and the road. There are many paths through the dunes; as long as you keep the sea to the left and the road to the right, a degree of flexibility is possible. The trail takes you past a shallow pond and a variety of plant life.

4. On reaching a narrow strip of tarmac half obscured by drifting sand which crosses the dunes, turn right along it, this leads down to the road, cross carefully, and head towards the roundabout.

5. As you reach the roundabout the rides of Pleasureland may be viewed in the distance. At the roundabout turn right down Weld Road, after about 200 yards the Fisherman's Rest is reached and a welcome pint. On leaving the pub continue down Weld Road, past the junction with Lulworth Road.

6. The Park Hotel soon comes into view, giving the opportunity for a pint while you await your train, as Birkdale railway station is only a few yards further along the road. A train can now take you back to Ainsdale station where you started the walk. Alternatively, if the weather is good and you have energy to burn, why not stroll back along the beach.

5. BURSCOUGH

Route: Burscough Bridge – Rufford – Ring O' Bells – Burscough

Distance: 8.5 miles

Map: OS Pathfinder 699 (1:25000) Chorley and Burscough Bridge

Start: Burscough Bridge Railway Station (SD444124)

Access: Burscough Bridge Railway Station has a direct link with Southport, for details of service phone BR on 051 709 9696. If arriving by car, parking space is available at the rear of the railway station, and there are several free car parks signed from the main street.

Ring O' Bells, Lathom (0704 893157)

The Ring O' Bells is located on the Leeds-Liverpool Canal near Lathom. It is a Boddingtons pub, serving Cains Mild and Boddingtons Bitter and a guest beer. The pub is fairly large with bars on two levels. Food is served at lunchtimes and evenings. It is worth noting that the pub is open all day Sundays for food, a useful feature after a long walk. Opening hours are 12.00 noon to 3.00 pm and 5.30 to 11.00 pm Monday to Saturday; on Sundays the pub is open 12.00 noon to 10.30 pm. Families are made welcome. There are tables outside, with a view of the canal.

The Ship, Lathom (0704 893117)

The Ship Inn is an extremely attractive country pub, just set back from the junction between the Rufford Branch of the Leeds-Liverpool Canal and the Canal proper. It sells Theakstons Best Bitter, Theakstons XB, Pendle Witches Brew and up to six guest beers. It is open 12.00 noon to 3.00 pm and 5.30 to 11.00 pm Monday to Friday; from 12.00 noon to 3.00 pm and 7.00 to 11.00 pm Saturday and Sunday. Food is served from 12.00 until 2.00 pm Monday to Saturday. The Ship Inn, not unsurprisingly, has a strongly nautical theme. Families are welcomed, and there is an outdoor drinking area.

The Ship

The Ship is known locally as the "Blood Tub": in the 1860s, when most local cottages kept their own pig, a landlady of the Ship Inn would offer free beer in return for a bucket of pig's blood, which she would turn into black puddings.

Burscough

Burscough is an agricultural community relying on typical rural pursuits for employment. It is also increasingly a dormitory town for Merseyside and Preston. It lies on the West Lancashire plain.

The Walk

1. The railway station exit takes you up a flight of steps onto a road bridge over the railway; turn left along the main road, then almost immediately left again down Red Cat Lane. After a few yards turn left again towards the railway station, then turn right along a footpath in front of the station building. The path is walled, with Johnson Haulage Contractors to the right. The path twists left then right to follow the railway line. At first, the grassy path is enclosed on both sides, however, the right-hand fence soon disappears and the walk follows the left-hand field boundary by the rail tracks.

2. At the end of the field turn right into Crabtree Lane. This is a very quiet lane, the level crossing has "do-it-yourself" gates which probably deter some motorists. Follow this lane as it bends through the fields; the lack of fences serves to make the walker feel part of the landscape.

3. At the end of the lane turn left onto Tarlscough Lane past Moss Farm to your left. This lane is wider, with a footway to the right-hand side, yet it too is almost devoid of traffic, though buses ply their route.

4. After a few hundred yards turn right at Curlew Farm down Curlew Lane. This, too, is a very narrow peaceful lane with fields to both sides, again largely unfenced. Follow the lane past the wonderfully named Tootle House Farm, where the lane changes its name to Tootle Lane. Continue along the lane as its name changes again to Brick Kiln Lane and crosses The Rufford Boundary Sluice.

5. Turn right at the main junction, along Holmeswood Road past a small school whose walls display its history. Turn left again at the Hesketh pub, cross the road and carry on past the attractive whitewashed Post Office.

6. Take the right-hand turn into the road signed to Parbold, the B5246. Follow the road as it curves rightwards past the attractive red brick of St Mary's Parish church. The road soon carries you over the Rufford Branch of the Leeds-Liverpool Canal. Carry on past the railway station and level crossing.

7. At the next bridge over the River Douglas, take the stile to the right and walk along the ridge to the right of the river. This attractive raised path permits good views of the surrounding countryside. Cross another stile and

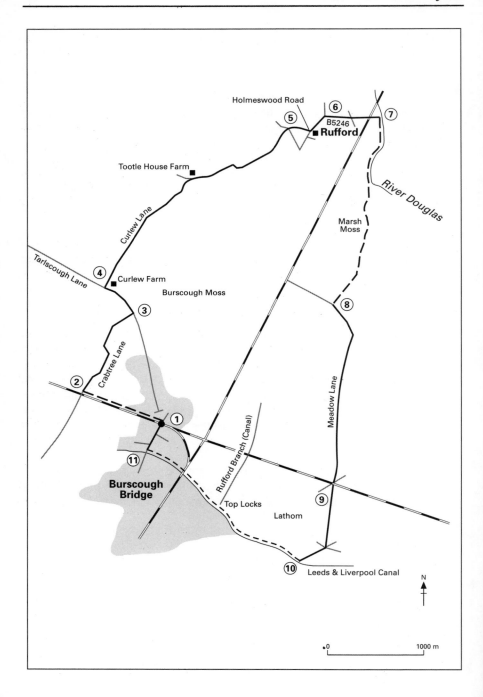

continue along the top of the ridge. The main branch of the river now bends away to the left, the walk continues along the top of the ridge which bears right along a narrow tributary. Ducks and the odd heron may appear. The fields to the left contain sheep while the fields to the right are cropped.

Keep with the ridge as it bears right, past a farm building on your left. Keep to the right of the stream. When we walked this path the only other people we saw were farmworkers, planting out young vegetables.

8. On reaching a road turn left to follow it, immediately crossing a bridge over the stream you have been following. There are open fields on either side and hills ahead. Follow the lane as it bends to the right and note the turf farm to the right with its acres of impeccable lawn.

9. Pass through the level crossing, remembering to shut the gate behind you if there is no signalman on duty. Take the left fork down Meadow Lane. At the next junction turn right onto Ring O' Bells Lane. The Ring O' Bells pub is soon reached giving the opportunity for a very welcome pint right next to the canal.

10. On leaving the pub turn right along the canal towpath, the path soon crosses a narrow wooden bridge which cars rattle as they cross. Continue along the canal, a farm to the right has pigs and piglets in runs adjacent to the path. An impressive stone bridge takes you over the Rufford Branch of the canal. The cluster of houses here, together with a flight of locks make a very pretty picture. The Ship Inn may be found to the right of the bridge. Continue along the canal, past ducks, narrow boats and an old mill building. The canal passes underneath a bridge carrying the railway.

11. At the next bridge take the steps up onto the road and turn right towards the Post Office. Burscough Bridge Railway Station is a few hundred yards further on. If you are waiting for a train, the Cambridge pub could not be in a better location, about 20 yards from the Southport-bound platform.

6. FORMBY POINT

Route: Freshfield – Formby Point – Formby

Distance: 6 miles

Map: OS Pathfinder 710 (1:25000) Formby and Maghull

Start: Freshfield Station (SD291083)

Access: Formby lies 8 miles north of Liverpool, and 4 miles south of Southport. Freshfield station is served by regular Merseyrail electric services from both Liverpool and Southport.

Train details from Merseytravel on 051 236 7676.

Freshfield lies 1 mile west of the A565, off the B5424. There is a large car park, for rail passengers only, next to Freshfield station.

Railway Hotel, Formby (0704 873024)

The Railway Hotel lies close to Formby Railway station. It has a separate public bar, and a large open lounge. Food is served at lunchtimes Monday to Friday, and at Sunday lunchtime. Children are welcome inside when eating, and there is a pleasant outdoor drinking area from which perfect views are obtained of the Merseyrail electric services entering and leaving Formby station. Tetley bitter is served here, along with one guest ale. Opening hours are 12.00 noon to 3.00 pm and 5.00 pm to 11.00 pm Monday to Thursday; 12.00 noon to 11.00 pm Friday and Saturday; normal opening hours on Sunday.

Formby

Formby is now very much an up-market coastal dormitory town serving the working populace of Merseyside. Its setting amid the coastal dunes gives it a frontier town aspect: man constantly battling against elements which threaten to engulf it. The name Formby means the "homestead of Forni".

Freshfield is a Northern suburb of Formby: the site of the present village was once known as Church Mere. The original township was buried by sand between 1750 and 1850. It is said that the area was then made suitable for cultivation by a Mr. Fresh, who laid topsoil over the whole area. When the land was built upon again, it was thus natural to name it Freshfield.

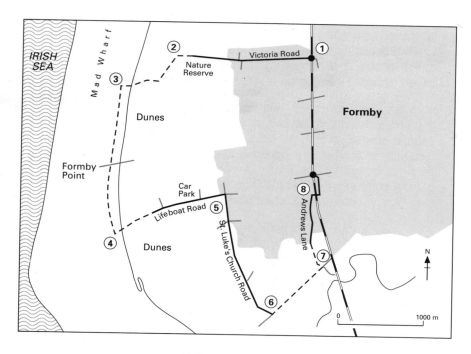

The Walk

1. From the car park turn right along Victoria Road and immediately cross the railway line. Walk along this attractive tree-lined road, passing Larkhill Lane to your left and passing into the Formby Point National Trust Nature Reserve. This is one of the major homes of the native British red squirrel. The red squirrel was once found all over the country, but is now to be found

only in its traditional pine heartlands in the north. The grey squirrel has replaced it in many parts of the country. It is worth deviating to the left from the road/path to wander around the reserve to view these most attractive animals, who will happily eat the nuts which you can purchase at the entrance. After watching these furry red critters return to the main pine tree-lined path/road and continue walking as far as the main large car park: this is some 500 yards further on.

2. Enter the car park and ignore the two sandy paths through the dunes ahead of you. Turn left instead along the marked bridleway: no permit is necessary for walkers! This is Nicotine Path, which skirts the site of a former tobacco waste tip. After 400 yards the path bends to the right and then to the left; a clearing opens up to your right, and here you should descend a steep dune to the beach. It does not matter too much exactly where you reach the beach, provided that you do at some stage!

3. Turn left along the beach, and enjoy the views of the Wirral Peninsula and the Welsh mountains beyond. If a southerly wind is blowing, you will find yourself blasted by both the wind and sand; you will be compensated by the fact that southerlies are generally quite mild, and by the beautiful sand patterns formed by the wind. Fences and shrubs have been erected to prevent dune erosion, and old Christmas trees have also been pressed into duty. You will pass an elaborate board-walk in the dunes to your left.

4. After about a mile of beach-walking you will come across the remains of the oldest lifeboat station in Britain dating from 1776. The building has now been demolished and is marked by the remains of red brick foundations and a plaque. Turn left here along Lifeboat Road; this is, of course, the old access road to the lifeboat station. The road is tarmac, but the dunes have covered much of the road and make walking quite difficult. Walk past Formby Point caravan park to your right.

5. On emerging from Lifeboat Road, turn right along a private roadway called St Luke's Church Road, and marked with a footpath sign. Carry on straight ahead past Alexandra Road. Your route comes into open countryside; continue past the bungalow to your right. Pass over the gravelled Rifle Road, and continue along your path which is designated here as the Sefton Coastal Footpath. Ensure that you keep the field immediately to your left behind barbed wire. You will probably be able to hear firing from the army

rifle range in the distance; don't worry you will turn off beforehand. Pass through a stile by a metal gate.

6. Turn left to keep along the Sefton Coastal footpath: the MOD firing range and training area is now to your right. Keep walking along the path towards the railway line: you will see Merseyrail electric trains which provide a very frequent and reliable service here.

7. At a wooden footpath sign, turn left along the field edge. (Note that the path has been moved 17 yards further on from the sign here, so that you walk around the field edge). The path bears you rightwards to the left of a ditch and towards some houses. On emerging from the path, continue straight ahead along Andrews Lane.

8. Turn right into Queens Road, passing over a level crossing. Note the beautiful red-door cottage immediately before the level crossing. Cross the road and turn left: the Railway public house lies on the corner on the left, at the end of this road. Pause here for refreshment before catching a Merseyrail train back to Freshfield: the journey only takes 2 minutes! Formby station is located opposite the Railway public house.

7. HIGHTOWN

Route: Hightown – Hall Road

Distance: 3 miles

Map: OS Pathfinder 710 (1:25000) Formby and Maghull

Start: Hightown Railway Station (SD300036)

Access: Hightown railway station is located on the Liverpool – Southport line which offers a frequent service. If travelling by car, take the A565 coast road and turn off onto the B5193 to Hightown.

The Hightown Hotel, Hightown (051 929 2500)

The Hightown Hotel is a large imposing building, complete with immaculate bowling green, right next door to the railway station. There are several bars on the ground floor and tables outside around the bowling green. The small Buffet Bar contains a wooden display board listing past presidents of the Blundellsands Bowling Club, back to 1910. Draught Bass is available on hand-pump. Snacks are available throughout the day. The Hightown is open all day Monday to Saturday (12 noon to 11.00 pm); normal Sunday hours apply. Families are welcomed, and there is an outside drinking area.

Hightown

Hightown is a small community at the mouth of the river Alt. The dunes are a haven for wildlife and very attractive especially in summer when they are alive with flowers. To the north lies the Altcar rifle range, so the initial phases of this walk might be accompanied by sounds of gunfire! The Alt is Merseyside's second largest river after the Mersey, draining much of the surface water from the north Liverpool conurbation. There are over 75 kilometres of rivers, streams and brooks within the catchment area of the river. A fascinating collection of personal reminicences about Hightown are contained in the booklet "My Hightown 1897-1969" by Joe Bulman, which is available from Sefton Libraries & Arts Services.

Sefton Coastline

The Walk

1. Exit Hightown Station on the side, where trains depart for Southport. Follow Alt Road, past the Hightown Hotel, to which you will return, turn right into School Road past the Post Office, then left down Lower Alt Road. Continue straight on past the roundabout and unusual brick war memorial until you reach the river. The sound of gunfire from Altcar Rifle Range gives a strange atmosphere to the otherwise calm streets.

2. Turn left past a short row of houses and then go through a stile and along a gravelled path above the river bank, this is part of the Sefton Coastal Path. Note the sentry box on the opposite bank of the Alt, displaying a red flag when firing is taking place on the range. The sands are soon visible as the river bends to the right and away from our path.

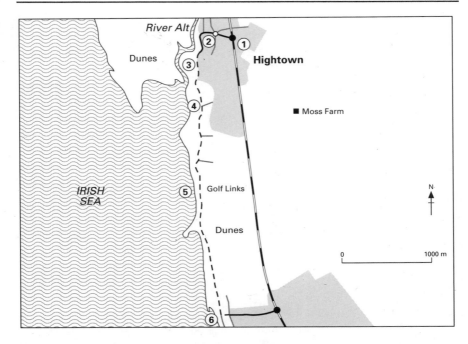

3. A wooden hut can be seen to the right, reached by following the gravel path to its end. This is a hide and a useful place to stop if you wish to watch the birds without them seeing you. However, the path bears right before reaching the hut, away from the gravelled path and into the dunes. From this point on follow the white marker poles which indicate the route through the dunes. There are several side tracks but the main path is usually clear, and the markers occur at regular intervals.

The dunes here are extremely rich in wildlife, the rare Natterjack Toad may be found. Birds of prey can be seen hovering above the dunes. In the summer there is a profusion of many different flowers, and butterflies.

4. Emerge from the dunes into the small car park of a sailing club, at this point a diversion may be made along a path signed to the submerged forest, which takes you down onto the river bank. The forest is difficult to identify at first, the submerged stumps and logs are covered in seaweed and strongly resemble rocks. Return to the car park and continue along the coastal path.

5. A yellow marker post soon directs you right towards the sea and then left

along a rough track, with the sea to your right and the West Lancashire Golf Course in the dunes to your left. The path takes you past what is at present a fenced-off building site, which is part of North West Water's effort to clean up the Mersey. The path continues alongside a temporary access road to the site.

6. The Coastguard Station soon becomes visible ahead. Pass through a stile and onto the Promenade. In front of the Coastguard Station there is a coin-operated telescope and a map, presented by the Soroptimists International of Crosby, identifying locations of interest that can be viewed from this point.

Immediately past the Coastguard Station turn left, continue down Hill Road West towards the Railway Station, and a train back to Hightown, where a well-deserved pint may be obtained in the Hightown Hotel.

8. SEFTON

Route: Sefton – Lunt – Lydiate – Sefton

Distance: 8 miles

Map: OS Pathfinder 710 (1:25000) Formby and Maghull

Start: Parish church of St Helen, Sefton (SD357013)

Access: Sefton Village lies just off the B5422, 1.5 miles west of Maghull, and just north-west of the motorway intersection between the M57 and the M58.

Bus services link Sefton Village with Maghull, Southport and Bootle. For full details of bus services, contact Merseytravel on 051 236 7676. Bus services stop outside the church.

St Helen's church is situated on Lunt Lane, Sefton; car parking is available down Sefton Mill Lane, by the church, and on-street in Brickwall Lane, opposite the church.

Scotch Piper, Southport Road, Lydiate
(051 526 0503)

This attractive thatched pub reportedly dates from 1320, making it the oldest inn in the old county of Lancashire. Fine ales are served from Burtonwood on gravity dispense. The pub retains a fine old world atmosphere. There are several small attractive rooms, and there is no formal bar counter. Most of the inn's original structural features have been retained. This is a pub genuinely unchanged through the centuries. Roaring fires welcome you in the winter.

There are tables outside and a children's play area. The Scotch Piper is open Monday to Saturday 11.30 am to 3.00 pm, and 5.30 pm to 11.00 pm. Normal Sunday opening hours apply. No food is served, but patrons are welcome to bring their own packed lunch. The name reputedly derives from an injured highland piper from the 1745 rebellion who took refuge at the inn, formerly known as the Royal Oak, and married the inn-keeper's daughter.

Running Horses, Bells Lane, Lydiate (051 526 3989)

This pleasant, multi-roomed canal-side pub serves a selection of ales from Peter Walker. Real fires greet you, and there is an outdoor beer garden right next to the canal and a children's adventure playground. Children are made welcome. Lunchtime food is served until 2.30 pm. The Running Horses is open all day (12.00 noon to 11.00 pm) Monday to Saturday; normal Sunday opening hours apply.

Leeds-Liverpool Canal at Bells Lane, Lydiate

Sefton

This small village gives its name to the District of Sefton: the word means an area or town where rushes grow. This is particularly appropriate given Sefton's low-lying position by the banks of the River Alt. The former Corn Mill has now been converted into attractive private dwellings. The church of St Helen has a quiet and attractive churchyard, accessed through a lych-gate off Sefton Mill Lane.

Lydiate

The village of Lydiate, which nowadays merges into Maghull, lies on the banks of the Leeds-Liverpool Canal. It is reached on this walk by taking the Maghull Hey Cop across Altcar Meadows. The name means "swing gate"; this is presumed to refer to a gate which would have been situated in the area to prevent cattle straying from pasture to arable land.

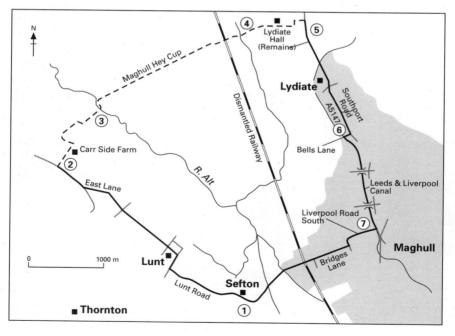

The Walk

1. From the church of St Helen, turn right along Lunt Lane and proceed northwards past the Punchbowl, which is next to the church. This pub may well provide you with a welcome source of refreshment at the end of the walk. For the time being, continue walking along the road as far as the hamlet of Lunt. Bear right with the road in Lunt, noticing the array of geese and free range chickens in the field to your left. Pass through the hamlet of Lunt following the road: Lunt means small wood or grove. As the road bends left, note the gateposts on the right, all that remains of Lunt Hall. Continue along what is now called East Lane. At the outskirts of Ince Blundell you will notice a curved red brick wall to your left; this encloses Ince Blundell Park and Hall. Walk further past a gateway on your left, and a former toll cottage on your right, which now houses an animal rescue centre.

2. At the next gateway on your left, cross over the road and take the footpath to Carr Side Farm, taking the opportunity to glance back towards Ince Blundell Hall. Go past all of the buildings as far as a metal gate in front of the final farm shed; pass over the stile to the left of the gate here, and follow the fence towards the coppice. Take care as the fence here is electrified! At the corner of the field, turn right and pass over two stiles. At the next field corner, turn right ignoring the wooden bridge to your left. After 100 yards, take the wooden bridge to your left over the drainage ditch, and make for the new metal bridge 250 yards ahead of you over the River Alt.

3. Scramble up the bank to reach this bridge; cross it and turn initially left, and then right in front of steel piping to follow a wide pathway over Maghull Hey Cop; the path runs to the right of the irrigation ditch. At the right time of year a selection of fauna can be spotted here: hares, ducks, bees, butterflies, grouse and pheasants. After 1.5 miles, cross over a stile to the right of a metal gate and continue straight on, crossing over a disused railway line: the white cottage to your right used to be Lydiate Station. Walk towards the road and pass over the wooden stile.

4. Take the footpath right over the fields which lies 20 yards to the left along the road. The path lies to the left of a stream. Continue straight along this path; a fence replaces the stream to your right. At the end of the field, turn left in the next field and follow the path around the edge of the coppice to your left towards Southport Road. Keep the ruins of St Katherine's Chapel in

view to your right. On reaching the road, look back into the coppice and you will see the ruins of Lydiate Hall.

5. Turn right along Southport Road past the remains of St Katherine's Chapel. Fifty yards further to your right lies the atmospheric and welcoming Scotch Piper inn. Continue south along the road, passing over the canal.

6. After one mile, turn right along Bells Lane. The Running Horses pub is next to the canal, just over a rickety bridge. Pause here for further refreshment. On leaving the pub turn right to follow the towpath of the Leeds-Liverpool Canal.

7. On reaching a distinctive stone bridge with a separate metal pedestrian bridge on either side, just beyond a new office building, pass under the bridge and then take the slope and steps to the right, though the gate and turn left onto Liverpool Road South. The road turns left through traffic lights, at the next set of lights turn right into Sefton Lane (B5422) towards Sefton. The road carries you over a bridge and past Roller Rink to the right. Bridges Lane, as the road soon becomes, returns the walker to the village of Sefton, and refreshment in the Punchbowl Inn, if required.

9. MELLING

Route: Melling – Melling Mount – Melling

Distance: 4.5 miles

Map: OS Pathfinder 710 (1:25000) Formby and Maghull

Start: Bootle Arms Public House, Melling (SD389002)

Access: Melling is situated 1 mile east of the interchange between the M57 and the M58. It lies 1 mile west of the A506.

Maghull railway station is served by Merseyrail and lies 1 mile west of the village centre. For details of bus and rail services contact Merseytravel on 051 236 7676.

There is car parking at the Bootle Arms for patrons only, and to the side of St Thomas' church. Alternatively there is plenty of on-street parking.

Pear Tree, Melling Mount

The Pear Tree is a country pub situated on the junction with the A506. When the authors visited, it served good ale from Cains and Greenalls. There is a pleasant atmosphere in the open-roomed interior, and there are some outside tables. Families are welcomed, and there is a good, reasonably-priced food menu. Food is served at lunchtimes, seven days a week. The pub is open all day Monday to Saturday, and normal Sunday opening hours apply.

Bootle Arms, Melling (051 526 2886)

The Bootle Arms is a country pub, within sight of the M57 and M58, yet managing to cater for local and walkers trade in the public bar, while catering for out-of-town eating in the large lounge and restaurant area. Food is served lunchtimes and evenings Monday to Saturday, and throughout the day on Sunday. There are coal fires and an outside drinking area, and children's amusement area. Families are welcomed; there is a family area. Ales from Burtonwood are served. The Bootle Arms is open 11.30 am to 11.00 pm Monday to Saturday, and between 12.00 noon and 10.00 pm on Sunday. (Please note that all day Sunday drinking only applies to those taking meals).

The Bootle Arms

Melling

Melling is a small village, formerly a mainly agricultural community, but now very much within the Merseyside commuter belt. It nevertheless retains its rural atmosphere despite its nearness to Maghull and Kirkby. Melling means "the people belonging to Moll", who is assumed to be an Anglo-Saxon chieftain. The church of St Thomas dates from 1616. Melling Mount is so-called as it lies at an elevation of over 100 feet!

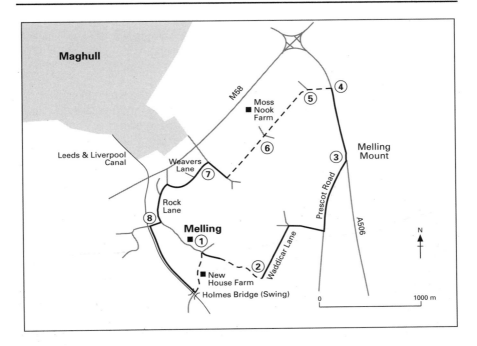

The Walk

1. From the Bootle Arms turn right along the road (Eastwards). Take the footpath to Waddicar Lane, which lies just to the left of a small red postbox. The path runs to the left-hand edge of a field; ignore the paths crossed to the left and right; continue onwards as the path becomes very narrow between a hedge to the left and a fence to the right. It then becomes a mini concrete causeway, and leads you to Waddicar Lane.

2. Turn left along Waddicar Lane. At the first junction, bear right with the main road. At the junction with Prescot Road, turn left and follow the road. Pass Angers Lane. At the junction with the A506 at Melling Mount — you are now over 100 feet high — the Pear Tree lies to your right.

3. After suitable refreshment at the pub, turn left along the Prescot Road and continue for half a mile.

4. Just before a barn building on the left selling farm produce, take notice of

the broken concrete stile on your left and the wooden waymarker post with the white top and yellow ring. Turn left here along a footpath, which takes the left-hand field margin, and keeps a stream on your left.

5. At the end of the field, cross over a small bridge by the waymarker post and into the very narrow Giddygate Lane. Cross the lane and rejoin the footpath by crossing a stile. The path goes through an overgrown area, but the path is clear and follows the line of the telegraph poles. A stile is soon reached which takes you into a wheat field, again follow the line of the telegraph poles which take you along the right-hand field margin, there is a drainage ditch to the right separating the two fields. A wooden bridge carries you over a drainage ditch at right angles to the path.

6. Cross over the road by the farm house and continue along the footpath which runs at the right hand edge of a field, keeping a hedge to your right. After 400 yards you will cross a small bridge and continue along a narrow path. On reaching the road turn right and walk towards the bridge over the M58.

7. Turn left into Weavers Lane, and after 500 yards, turn left again into Rock Lane. This road will lead you quickly uphill into the village of Melling and to the Bootle Arms.

8. Alternatively turn right into Brewery Lane towards the bridge over the Leeds-Liverpool Canal. Cross the bridge and immediately duck left through the white fencing, and take the steep steps down to the towpath. Follow the canal for half a mile to the south-east (right) here, and you will enjoy a good view of St Thomas' church to the left, and towards Aintree on your right. Take note of the marker post showing that you are 116 miles from Leeds, and 11 miles from Liverpool. Note that this canal towpath is not an official public footpath, but is a generally used right of way. At the black and white swing bridge, cross the canal and follow the path through New House Farm back to the start of the walk, giving you an opportunity to enjoy well-deserved refreshment in the Bootle Arms.

10. CROSBY

Route: Waterloo – Crosby Promenade – Crosby

Distance: 3 miles

Map: OS Pathfinder 721 (1:25000) Wallasey

Start: Waterloo Railway Station (SJ 321981)

Access: Waterloo lies on the Merseyrail Northern electric services; for details contact Merseytravel on 051 236 7676. Blundellsands and Crosby is the next station northwards on the Northern Line.

Waterloo lies a quarter of a mile west of the A565; follow signs to the free car park behind Waterloo Station.

The Warren Bar, La Barbacoa, Crosby (051 924 0445)

The Warren Bar is large, comfortable and roomy. The regular beers available include Castle Eden and Flowers. Guest beers are also available, when we visited these were West Country Pale Ale and Pompey Royal. Generously-portioned meals are served in the bar and there is a very pleasant dining area, almost a conservatory. Opening times are 12 noon to 3 pm and 7 pm to 12 midnight; note that the bar is closed on Monday lunchtimes. Normal Sunday hours apply.

Waterloo

Waterloo is a Northern suburb of the Liverpool conurbation, at the Southern end of the dune-clad Sefton coastline. This suburb takes its name from the Royal Waterloo Hotel, named after the famous battle of 1815. This link was lost when the name of the hotel was shortened to the Royal Hotel.

Dunes near Crosby

Crosby

Crosby means the "village with crosses", and refers to the neighbouring villages of Great and Little Crosby. Six stone crosses are still in situ at Little Crosby.

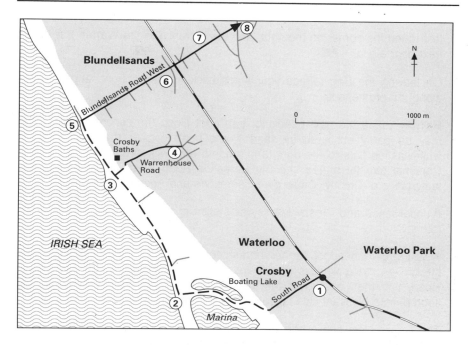

The Walk

1. From Waterloo Station, walk towards the boating lake and the sea along South Road. Note the figurehead on the frontage of the Marine public house to your right. Cross over Marine Terrace, and bear diagonally right after the toilet block. Pass over the site of a new road, and take the path which leads between the boating lake and Crosby Marina. If it's stormy on the sea, the sea-birds will be sheltering here; you may spot a cormorant if you are lucky!

2. On reaching the beach turn right along Crosby Promenade. There are views to the left over to New Brighton on the Wirrál, and to the mountains of North Wales beyond. Beware the sandstorms which high winds will whip up into your face along the promenade.

3. Just before a slipway down to the beach, turn right along a path inland, with Crosby baths to your left. The path becomes Warrenhouse Road; follow the road, bearing right when it forks. Pass the Royal Oak to your left and take the next turning to the right into Bridge Road. La Barbacoa Restaurant is

just round the corner on the right, and the entrance to the Warren Bar is the next door along.

4. On leaving the Bar, retrace your steps back to the seafront, and continue along the promenade.

5. Halfway round the next headland, turn right along the concrete path – this may be partly obscured by sand – and bear towards the road between whitewashed flats to the right, and modern red brick apartments to the left. Continue straight ahead into Blundellsands Road West. Walk through the leafy lanes of Crosby. Cross over Serpentine and Agers Road.

6. Blundellsands and Crosby Merseyrail station is soon reached for the return journey.

7. If you are in need of further refreshment, take the underpass and walk straight on along what is now Blundellsands Road East. Cross over Eshe Road, and then pass over the junction into Victoria Road West. You will soon pass a pleasant little lagoon to the left, replete with coots and ducks.

8. The Crows Nest public house lies a further 100 yards along Victoria Road on the left. Pause here to enjoy fine ale and a timeless atmosphere. Retrace your steps to Blundellsands and Crosby station, and catch one of the frequent Merseyrail electric services back to Waterloo.

11. RAINFORD

Route: Rainford Junction – Crawford – Kings Moss – Rainford Junction

Distance: 6.5 miles

Map: OS Pathfinder 711 (1:25000) Wigan and Ormskirk

Start: Rainford Junction Railway Station (SD478026)

Access: Rainford Junction railway station lies one mile north-east of the village of Rainford. Car parking is available in the car park by the station.

A regular rail service links Rainford Junction with Wigan and Liverpool; for service details contact Merseytravel on 051 236 7676.

Colliers Arms, Kings Moss (0744 892894)

The Colliers Arms is a pleasant village pub in the hamlet of Kings Moss. There are several separate drinking areas inside, along with a beer garden and tables in front of the pub. Children are welcome, and there is a family area. The pub has recently been renovated but retains much of its original character with stone floors and roaring open fires. You can enjoy extremely good beer from Greenalls. Good food is served every lunchtime between 12.00 noon and 2.00 pm, and between 5.00 pm and 9.00 pm Wednesday to Saturday, between 7.00 pm and 9.00 pm Sundays. As suggested by its name, the Colliers Arms displays many mining memorabilia reflecting the former dominant industry in the area.

Crawford Arms, Crawford (0744 882421)

The Crawford Arms is a very lively pub, which welcomes families and serves good food from an extensive and interesting menu. There is a family room, and an outdoor drinking area. Excellent hand-pumped ale is served from Greenalls. There is a real fire inside the pub, and an outside drinking area and playground. The Crawford Arms truly forms a social centre for the village of Crawford.

The Crawford Arms is open 12.00 noon to 11.00 pm Monday to Saturday; normal Sunday opening hours apply. Food is available throughout the day Monday to Saturday until 9.30 pm. On Sundays food is available 12.00 noon till 2.30 pm, and from 7.00 pm to 9.30 pm.

Rainford

Rainford is a small commuter village, the name meaning "the ford by a boundary strip", which may relate to the point at which the road through the mosslands to the village crosses the Sankey Brook.

Crawford

Crawford is a one street village, possibly the last one-street former mining village in the country, its name deriving from the Earl of Crawford, a Wigan landowner, who owned the mine which once spawned the village. The attractive Methodist Chapel once formed the focal centre of village life: all social, educational and religious activities took place here. Crawford truly deserves the description of a timeless Lancashire village.

Kings Moss

Kings Moss is a tiny rural hamlet. Now a mainly agricultural community, although the area has strong mining links, and this history is reflected in the photographs on the walls of the Colliers Arms (and, indeed, in the name itself!).

The Walk

1. Take the footpath leading eastwards which commences directly to the south of the bridge, and opposite the car park entrance. The path leads along the left-hand edge of a cropped field; the railway runs parallel to your left. Pass the gap in the hedgerow and continue. Go past the first bridge over the railway.

2. At the second bridge over the railway line, turn left up the steps at the end of the field, and turn left to cross the bridge. Turn right almost immediately to follow the path; now the path takes the right-hand field edge and the railway is to your right.

3. At the next field boundary, turn ninety degrees to your left to walk between the fields. Be careful here as the hedge marking the field boundary no

longer exists. There is a small marker post with a yellow arrow to guide you attached to the fence on your right. After about 75 yards you will be level with the first of a row of trees on your right, and with the first pylon beyond the trees. Turn right here and head straight across the field, following the footpath alignment. Take care again, because the path is not immediately obvious. Aim straight for the first tree and the pylon, and you will find that the path develops into a grassed embankment. Continue to ·head towards the pylon. The paths bears leftward of the pylon, and then sharper left around an ICI valve compound.

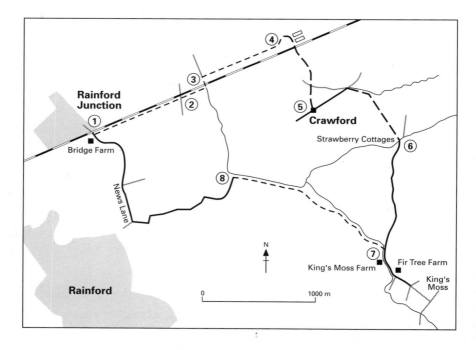

4. At the path junction, bear right in front of the row of pressure containers and make for the railway line. Cross the railway line: take care and look both ways before crossing. Continue straight on, and then slightly rightwards towards the village of Crawford. At the main road, the Crawford Arms lies across the road to your right; the Methodist Chapel lies 100 yards down the road to your right.

5. Turn eastwards along the village main street to continue your walk (left from the footpath, or right from the Crawford Arms). At the end of the village street, take the footpath signposted to your right along the left edge of a field. This lies opposite an executive housing development. The path bears rightwards towards Strawberry Cottage.

6. At the road, turn right and walk one mile into the village of Kings Moss, passing both Strawberry Cottage and then Kings Moss Farm to your right. The Colliers Arms lies on your right on the village main street. On leaving the Colliers Arms, retrace your steps as far as Kings Moss Farm.

7. Take the footpath leftwards just beyond the farm. The Black Brook on your right forms the county boundary here between Merseyside and Greater Manchester. The path follows the right-hand field margin. Pass the caravan lot to your right, and pass through a wooden gate. Follow the track which leads you after half a mile to a road.

8. Turn left here past two white houses on the opposite side of the road. After half a mile, turn right at the road junction into News Lane, ignoring Hydes Brow to your left. This pleasant road leads you after three quarters of a mile to Rainford Junction Station, where you commenced the walk. The Old Stables public house lies to the right on the Northern side of the bridge, should you need to wait for a train.

12. BILLINGE

Route: Billinge – Billinge Hill – Billinge

Distance: 4.5 miles

Map: OS Pathfinder 711 (1:25000) Wigan and Ormskirk

Start: Brown Cow Public House, Rainford Road, Billinge (SJ528000)

Access: Rainford Road, Billinge, is the B5205. The Brown Cow lies 50 yards along Rainford Road from its junction with the A571.

Billinge lies 5 miles north-east of St Helens; 4 miles South-west of Wigan. Good bus services link Billinge with St Helens and Wigan. Bus stops are situated at the junction between the A571 and Rainford Road. For service details contact Merseytravel on 051 236 7676.

Car parking is difficult in Billinge; there is limited on-street parking.

Holt's Arms, Crank Road, Billinge (0695 622705)

This very ancient inn lies at the foot of an old causeway route across the moss to Liverpool. At one stage it was owned by the shipowning Holt family of Liverpool, which accounts for its name. It is also known locally as the "Foot o' Causeway". Part of the grade 2 listed building dates from the 15th Century, with later additions in the 16th and 17th Centuries.

It has recently been renovated very successfully, and much of the original wooden panelling has been incorporated in the decor. There is an outdoor drinking area, a children's room, and real fires. A fine bowling green stands at the rear. This pub serves an excellent pint of Burtonwood bitter. The Holt's Arms is open all day Monday to Saturday (opening at 12.00 noon); on Sunday normal opening hours apply. Food is available every lunchtime 12.00 noon to 2.30 pm.

Billinge

Billinge is a straggling former mining community, situated on the very edge of Merseyside. There are two suggested derivations for the place-name: either, from the Old English for sword or edge, hence 'prominent hill'; or, from the Old English personal name Billa, hence 'the people belonging to Billa'.

View from the heights of Billinge Hill

The Walk

1. From the Brown Cow pub, walk further west along Rainford Road. Pass Edleston Fields on your left, a field sports facility for the people of Billinge.

2. Turn right up a private road and footpath marked "no vehicular access for the general public". This road leads initially towards Crookhurst Farm. Follow the road/footpath, as it swings left before the farm. Continue to climb. Gradually an extensive vista opens up on all sides.

3. At the brow of the hill take the footpath off to the left of the road, while the road corkscrews to the right. Pass over some stone blocks, and continue straight on following the left-hand field margin. Cross over a footpath, and continue onwards towards the radio mast. Continue to the left of this mast, and then to the left of Beacon Farm, a newish stone house.

4. At the junction with Crank Road, turn right and descend the hill. You will pass the grounds of Bispham House on your left, which is now a scouting centre. After half a mile you will come upon the attractive and welcoming Holt's Arms.

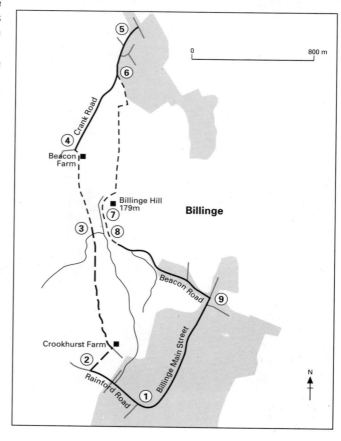

5. After suitable refreshment, leave the pub and retrace your steps part-way up Crank Road.

6. Just after Coleridge Road, take the footpath on your left, indicated by a line of stone flags. This path soon leads rightwards through an attractive coppice. Follow the path as it runs rightwards through the coppice. Continue rightwards as far as a wooden gate; pass through this, and turn immediately left along the left-hand edge of a field. The path leaves the field, returning into the coppice. Pass through the metal gate into land owned by the Woodland Trust. Go straight through the heart of the coppice. Start to ascend gradually within the wood, taking the right-hand way and continuing straight on, keeping the radio masts to your right. You will glimpse a brick tower through the trees ahead of you: this is the summit of Billinge Hill. Make towards this, passing through the metal pedestrian gate, marking the end of the Woodland Trust's land through which our footpath travels. Follow the path as it bears successively upwards and to the right. Then continue straight on, leaving the green mesh fence behind you and to the left. The path bears left towards the tower, and then rightwards and around the tower.

7. There is no official right of way to the tower, known as "Billinge Beacon" and first built as a summer house, but locals traditionally use it as a wonderful vantage point for the whole area. At 179 metres this is one of the highest points in Merseyside. A succession of differing landscapes and counties is laid out in front of you: on a clear day you can see Merseyside, Greater Manchester, Lancashire, Cheshire, Staffordshire, Clwyd and Gwynedd. The vista provides a wonderful contrast of peaks and plains, of industry and countryside. Resume the path around the summit of Billinge Hill, and follow it downwards keeping the green wire mesh fence to your left. Ignore the path to your right, and continue to bear left and down alongside the fence.

8. When you reach the road, turn left, cross over it, and take the footpath downwards on the other side between gorse bushes. This path bears round to the left, and then runs to the immediate right of a wire mesh fence, while a cropped field and Billinge drop away to your right. The path becomes paved, widens into a roadway, and then becomes Beacon Road. Follow it until it meets the A571, Billinge Main Street.

9. Turn right here and follow the road downhill for one mile through Billinge as

far as the junction with Rainford Road and the Brown Cow. There are bus stops along the length of this road, which can be used to return to Wigan or St Helens. There is a succession of interesting buildings as you pass through Billinge: the church of St Aidan's, dating from 1718 with an attractive bell tower, clock-face and weather-vane; a curious petrol station on the right, set apparently in someone's front garden, and a minuscule telephone exchange on the left. If you can't wait for refreshment, you can try the Forester's Arms, halfway down the hill on your left; a good locals' pub, which serves enjoyable Burtonwood beer.

13. CRANK

Route: Crank – Windle – Moss Bank – Carr Mill Dam – Crank

Distance: 6 miles

Map: OS Pathfinder 722 (1:25000) St Helens and Huyton-with-Roby

Start: Red Cat Public House, Crank (SJ503998)

Access: Regular bus services connect the village of Crank with Billinge and St Helens; contact Merseytravel on 051 236 7676 for full service details.

Crank is situated 2 miles south-west of Billinge, 4 miles north-east of St Helens town centre. The village lies 1.5 miles north of the A580, East Lancs Road. Parking exists at the Red Cat for patrons only; otherwise there is parking on-street.

Black Horse, Moss Bank (0744 23847)

This is the highest pub in St Helens. It is a pleasant stone building with a lively bar and three lounge areas. Some cheap lunchtime snacks can be obtained. Families are welcomed in the outdoor beer garden, where there is also a bowling green. Real ales served are Greenalls mild and bitter, and Stones bitter. The Black Horse is open 12.00 noon to 4.00 pm, and 7.00 pm to 10.30 pm Monday to Friday; it is open all day Saturday from 12.00 noon to 11.00 pm; normal Sunday hours apply.

Crank

Crank is a small isolated hamlet in the rural hinterland of St Helens.

Windle

The Parish of Windle means "windy hill", subtly alluding to the fact that this is one of the higher spots of St Helens. Locals jokingly refer to Windle as Windle City, as they believe inhabitants have constantly exaggerated its importance.

Moss Bank

Moss Bank means "the ridge by mossland". The ridge rises to over 250 feet, with Reeds Moss to the west and Carr Mill to the right. The highest pub in St Helens is situated here (see above).

Carr Mill Dam

This was one of the foremost tourist attractions of the North West, rivalling Southport and Blackpool. Charabancs of tourists would arrive at Carr Mill and queue to pass through its turnstiles, so great was its pull for leisure pursuits. Stories abound about Carr Mill Dam, for example, it is rumoured to be bottomless. During the Second World War the Luftwaffe used Carr Mill Dam as a navigation aid during their bombing raids, turning west to bomb the ports of Liverpool, and east along the East Lancs Road to bomb the industrial might of Manchester. Carr also means "marsh" in Old Norse.

The Walk

1. The walk commences from the Red Cat Inn on Red Cat Lane in the hamlet of Crank. Take the road, Higher Lane, immediately opposite the pub entrance and bear gently downhill and then rightwards with the road.

2. At the junction with Mill Lane turn left and continue along the road as you pass light industrial units on either side of the road. Do not be discouraged at this point; the walk will soon assume a gentle rural aspect. Pass over Rainford Brook.

3. Turn left into Berrington's Lane, following the footpath sign immediately beyond a stone house on your left. Square Wood will be passed to your

right; it truly lives up to its name. Continue along Berrington's Lane for a mile until its junction with Crank Road: this brings you into the Parish of Windle.

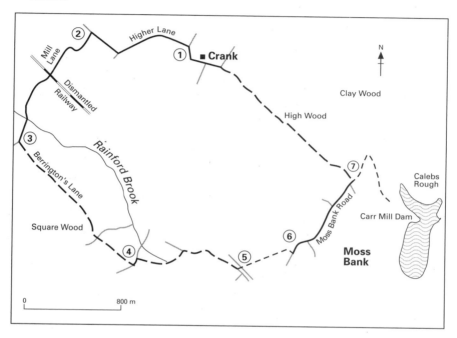

4. Turn left along Crank Road; after 50 yards take the footpath to the right along Sandy Lane. The track bears leftwards away from the house on your right. Cross over the bridge and turn rightwards with the path. The path twists alternately left then right, running along with fields on both sides.

5. Before the first house, take the footpath left and almost immediately bear diagonally rightwards across the field towards the houses. Ignore the grass track to the left. Pass over a stile; the track continues to bear upwards diagonally across the field towards a wooden fence. (A sign at the stile advises walkers to walk along the edges of the field as bulls may be grazing; exercise your own judgement and caution here. When the authors visited the field was empty and they were able to follow the diagonal line of the footpath. If you are wary about bulls, retrace your steps back to the first house; turn left along the lane, and then left up Moss Bank Road; after 300

yards of ascent you will arrive where you would have exited the footpath across the field). Leave the field over a wooden stile to the right in the middle of a wooden fence. Pass along the narrow passageway.

6. Turn left up Moss Bank Road, passing the post office, and then reaching the Black Horse public house, where you can take some well deserved refreshment. Continue up the hill.

7. Take the path to the left, just before a bus stop. This path lies opposite no. 158. (Alternatively, to visit Carr Mill Dam, go over the brow of the hill, descend to the road junction; turn right and take the first footpath left: this brings you to Carr Mill Dam, where you may rest a while enjoying the evocative names of Caleb's Rough, Otter's Swift and Tanyard Ho. Retrace your steps to the footpath by the bus stop on Moss Bank Road, opposite house no. 158).

On the path there are views to the right towards Billinge Hill. Pass over the stile in a wooden gate, and take the track to the right of all the farm buildings. Pass over a further stile, and continue along an attractive narrow path. You will pass Clay Wood over the fields to your right. By High Wood the path descends, and then bears upwards again becoming a track in the middle of fields. Disused quarries lie in the copse to your right. At the brow of the hill continue straight on, and descend gently with the path towards Crank. Turn left at the road, admiring the tiny chapel to your right. Follow the road as it leads you through Crank, and bends to the right returning you to the Red Cat Inn.

14. BLACKBROOK

Route: Ship Inn – St Helens Canal – Haydock – Stanley Bank – Ship Inn

Distance: 3.5 miles

Map: OS Pathfinder 722 (1:25000) St Helens and Huyton-with-Roby

Start: Ship Inn, Blackbrook Road, St Helens (SJ535966)

Access: Buses serve Blackbrook Road; the stop is on the bridge next to the pub. By road, Blackbrook Road forms part of the A58, with access via the main East Lancashire Road (A580) turning off for Stanley Bank, or take the A58 from the Prescot exit of the M57. Parking space is available behind the pub, by the Sankey Valley Visitors Centre, where useful visitors' guides about the Sankey Valley Country Park may be obtained.

The Ship Inn, Blackbrook (0744 26494)

The Ship Inn located right next to the St Helens Canal is a very pleasant pub with a relaxed atmosphere. There is a large, yet cosy lounge and a smaller bar. The real ales include Greenalls Mild and Bitter, both on good form when we visited. Youngs Bitter and Stones Bitter are also normally available. The bar menu is quite extensive, and the coffee excellent. Food is available every lunchtime 12.00 noon to 2.00 pm. Families are welcomed, and there is a large beer garden. The Ship Inn is open all day Monday to Saturday (12.00 noon to 11.00 pm); normal Sunday hours apply.

Blackbrook

The Blackbrook area of St Helens is predominantly urban and residential, with a rich industrial heritage. The St Helens Canal or Sankey Navigation is one of the oldest canals in the country, completed in 1757. It provided the catalyst for industrial growth in the St Helens area: prior to the construction of the canal the only access to St Helens from the port of Liverpool was by road, often little better than a track, and freight had to be carried using horse and cart. The canal allowed coal dug in St Helens to be exported quickly – by the standards of the day – to Liverpool. Industrial development also took place in St Helens, as both raw materials and finished products could now be moved more easily, giving a competitive advantage.

Bridge over the Old Double Lock, Sankey Valley

The Walk

The walk takes you along part of the St Helens Canal, through local farmland, and, inevitably in an urban area, there is some road walking.

1. From the Ship Inn cross Blackbrook Road, and head towards the road bridge over the canal to your right. To the left of this bridge is the access to the canal, follow the path alongside the water. This is the Blackbrook branch of the canal which served to accommodate overflow from Car Mill Dam. A

footbridge over the canal is soon visible, beneath it lies a very small weir, with a drop of only a few inches. The open water here provides a home or resting place for ducks and an impressive display of bulrushes.

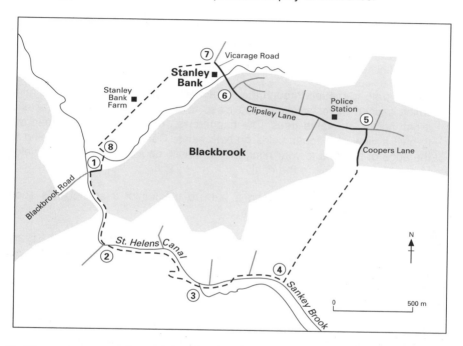

2. The water course bears left; take the footbridge over the canal, and turn left to follow the main St Helens Canal. The cascade of water, viewed from the bridge, covers the remains of the oldest double locks in the country. This was constructed at the same time as the rest of the canal (1756-57) and rebuilt in 1885, enabling the canal to serve certain local collieries.

The canal is now almost completely overgrown, buried in bulrushes and flowers, a very attractive sight in summer. Broad Oak Wharf, once a loading point serving the Broad Oak Collieries is soon reached. There is no water in it now and only the deviation in the stone banking to go around it tells you what was once there – though three old Mersey Flats (canal barges) lie buried here. Jump down from the wharf (about 2 feet) and continue along the canal bank.

3. Cross a green metalled bridge and continue along the left bank of the canal. The bushes and trees to the left surround the site of Frog Hall, now gone, a strangely named cottage. A plank bridge carries the path over a tiny stream. Engine Lock lies to the right on the canal, and the site of a swing bridge can be seen, which was once used by miners to reach Southport Colliery.

   Water may now be glimpsed on both sides of the path, the so-called flashes on the left result from mining subsidence.

4. Take a path to the left through the Havannah Flashes (named after the mine which caused them by mining too close to the surface): our path takes a slight incline into some trees. The hedgerows on either side soon open out to give a view of cropped fields on both sides. Carry straight on, keeping to the edge of the field to your right; the path rises above the level of the fields to give an open view to the right.

   Pass through a gate and along a path to the left of a school, this soon becomes the paved Coopers Lane.

5. At the end of the lane turn left into Clipsley Lane, passing Haydock Library and High School. Continue past the Waggon and Horses to the left.

6. At the mini roundabout take the right fork, and continue down Vicarage Road for a few hundred yards.

7. Turn left into Stanley Bank Road, this is also marked by a footpath sign, somewhat obscured by vegetation. This road soon becomes a path across open fields. The path takes the walker past the buildings of Stanley Bank Farm, where you might be lucky enough to spot a peacock or two: try looking at the roofs of the outbuildings.

8. At the end of this path turn left along a short stretch of track which, most conveniently, deposits you right outside the Ship Inn.

15. BURTONWOOD

Route: Earlestown – Sankey Valley – Burtonwood – Earlestown

Distance: 4.5 miles

Map: OS Pathfinder 722 (1:25000) St Helens and Huyton-with-Roby

Start: Earlestown Railway Station (SJ579952)

Access: Earlestown is situated 1.5 miles south-west of the M6 junction with the East Lancs Road. Limited on-street parking is available around the station. (Alternatively the walk can be started in Burtonwood, where more on and off-street parking is available.)

Earlestown station is served by a regular Merseyrail service; details from Merseytravel on 051 236 7676.

The Bridge Inn, Burtonwood (0925 225709)

The Bridge Inn is a pleasant multi-roomed pub, serving good beer from the local Burtonwood brewery. Admire the rugby memorabilia in the public bar; a reminder of the publicans illustrious sporting career. Otherwise relax in the saloon bar, or the new elevated family room. There is also an outdoor drinking area, a children's playground, and even a bowling green. The Bridge is open all day Monday to Saturday (11.30 am to 11.00 pm), and normal Sunday hours apply. Food is available between 12.00 and 2.00 pm.

Burtonwood

There was a large forest in the area around the 14th century; later the area became associated with the large USAF and RAF bases sited here. Many Burtonwood Brides emigrated to the States after the War with their GIs. It is now a compact, lively village: the famous Forshaws (Burtonwood) Brewery lies to the north of the village centre, and provides useful employment for many villagers.

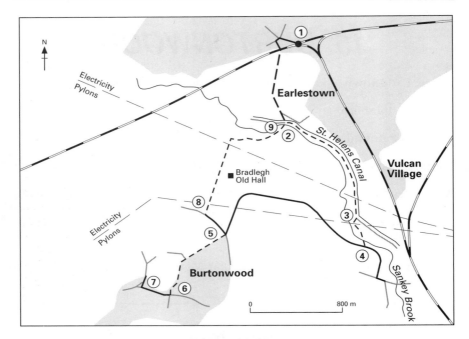

The Walk

1. From Earlestown Station turn left towards the Rams Head public house in Earle Street. Pass left in front of the Rams Head; then turn left up Junction Lane, following signs for Arends International, and pass over the railway bridge. Walk past the factories of Jenkinson to the right, and Shawtons to the left; turn immediately left behind Shawtons into the road with metal railings on either side. The road bends to the right; cross over to the front of Arends International, and take the footpath/pavement, as it bears leftwards and downwards. Continue straight ahead until you reach the St Helens Canal. Cross over the green bridge here.

2. Turn immediately left and walk along the canal towpath, which is often thronged with fishermen. The Sankey Brook, after which this valley walk is named, lies over the field to your right. Walk along the towpath for half a mile or so, past the lock by Vulcan Village, which has now been filled in, and makes the canal unnavigable. If you look to the back and leftwards here, you will see Vulcan Village, formerly founded on the rubber industry, spread out to view. Pass under one set of electric pylons.

Vulcan Village

3. Fifty metres before the next pylons, and before a canal bend to the left, take the path down and to your right over the fields. The path bends to the left. Cross over a farm track and pass over a narrow wooden footbridge with white metal railings.

4. When you meet the narrow lane, turn right. (Alternatively, if you wish to sample the delights of the wonderfully named pub, Fiddle i' th' Bag, turn left and walk 100 yards to the main road, Alder Lane). This delightful narrow lane leads after about a mile to the village of Burtonwood. Enjoy the dappled sunlight breaking through the trees lining the lane. Bear left with the lane on the approaches to Burtonwood. At the end of the lane, cross over the road, making for the footpath to the left of a white gate.

5. Turn down this footpath which will lead you to the village centre. Initially keep the houses to your left, and the cropped field to your right. The path bears to the left; keep the houses to your left. Cross the road and keep straight on. Pass down and then left over a small bridge.

6. At the main road, turn right and pass the Parish Hall to your left, and the church to your right.

7. Turn to the right at the Elm Tree; the Bridge Inn lies immediately behind this public house. After suitable refreshment, retrace your steps to the footpath, and then back along the footpath to the outskirts of Burtonwood. At the end of the footpath, turn left along Lumber Lane, ignoring the road opposite which you previously exited. You will pass the attractive red brick house called Brantwood to your left, built in 1902.

8. After a further 75 yards, turn right at the footpath signed over the field before the pylons. Follow the line of the telegraph poles and keep to the right-hand field margin. Note that the path may be overgrown with grass here. At the end of the field pass over/by the overgrown stile, and continue straight on along the right-hand edge of the field. Pass under a set of pylon wires, and then 50 yards later turn right along the field margin. Take care not to enter the cropped field ahead of you, but take time to admire the fine railway viaduct. The path here may also be overgrown with grass. Pass out of the field, and continue straight ahead along the well-delineated cinder track.

9. On reaching the red bridge over the Sankey Brook, cross over the river, and then pass straight on and over the green painted bridge over the St Helens Canal. Pass straight on and upwards, returning to Earlestown Station.

Alternatively, if starting and completing the walk in Burtonwood, do not cross the green bridge, but turn right along the towpath along the St Helens Canal. See paragraph (2) onwards above.

16. RAINHILL

Route: Rainhill – Sutton Manor – Rainhill

Distance: 4 miles

Map: OS Pathfinder 722 (1:25000) St Helens and Huyton-with-Roby

Start: Rainhill Railway Station (SJ492914)

Access: Rainhill Station is situated 1 mile north of Junction 7 of the M62. There is a free public car park opposite the station, and one behind the shopping centre.

Rainhill is served by a regular Merseyrail service: contact Merseytravel on 051 236 7676 for full details.

Coach and Horses, Rainhill

The Coach and Horses is a pleasant, recently refurbished pub, selling beers from Cains and Higsons. A glass conservatory acts as a sun trap. There are some seats outside. Food is served Mondays to Fridays between 12.00 noon and 2.30 pm, and between 5.00 and 7.30 pm.

The Commercial, Rainhill (051 426 6446)

The Commercial is a multi-roomed drinking house, serving beers from Cains, Higsons, Tetley and Theakstons. There is a small beer garden. Snacks are available at lunchtimes. The Commercial is open all day Monday to Saturday (11.30 am to 11.00 pm); on Sunday normal hours apply.

Rainhill

Rainhill was the setting for the famous Rainhill Trials, which were won by Stephenson's Rocket and provided an early test for rail travel in the world.

The Walk

The first 1.5 miles of this walk follow attractive paths through fields; the footpaths on the second half of the walk have unfortunately been recently obscured by a slag heap and light industrial units. The second half of the walk therefore is characterised by road walking, but along fairly quiet roads.

If you do not wish any road walking, the authors suggest walking as far as point (3) in the text, and then retracing your steps to Rainhill and well-deserved refreshment in the two excellent pubs there. Alternatively, you may catch a bus from Sutton Manor to return you to Rainhill. (Details from Merseytravel on 051 236 7676).

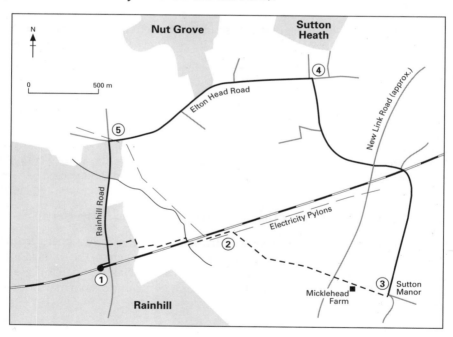

1. Starting from the Commercial, opposite Rainhill Station, pass over the railway footbridge into Rainhill Road. Turn immediately right before the Coach and Horses into Ritherup Lane. Bear right with this lane, which

becomes rutted, and then bear left of the blue fence of a waste paper plant. The path bears successively right and left towards a footbridge over the railway line. Pass up and over this bridge, and continue to walk along the edge of a field, parallel to the railway line.

2. Midway between the first two electricity pylons, the path bears diagonally right across the field. The field is cropped, but the line of the path is easily recognisable. Pass over a wooden stile at the end of the field, and follow the path as it snakes over the next grassy field around a bush. Go through the metal gate at the end of the field, and walk straight on towards the pylon, keeping to the left-hand edge of the field. Pass through a wooden gate, and pass down and cross over the new Link Road (take care here!). Go through the wooden gate on the other side of the Link Road, and walk straight on, passing Micklehead Farm.

3. Turn left into Lea Green Road. Walk past the Siemens, Osram, Rank Xerox industrial units, and the electricity sub-station. Walk up and over the rail bridge, and turn left. Pass under the new Link Road, and keep straight on along the grassy verge past Fog Centre, Linkway Automart and Tom's Gym.

4. At the top of the hill turn left into Elton Head Road. Look out for the collection of red telephone boxes on your right after a couple of hundred yards.

5. After half a mile turn left into Rainhill Road opposite the Black Horse public house, which sells Greenalls beers. After a further half mile, you will come to the Coach and Horses in Rainhill, where you may pause awhile. Cross over the railway footbridge and turn right to bring you back to the Commercial, another watering hole, and the start point of this walk.

17. LIVERPOOL AND BIRKENHEAD

Route: Liverpool – Albert Dock – Birkenhead – Birkenhead Priory – Liverpool

Distance: 5 miles

Map: Liverpool A-Z Street Atlas

Start: Liverpool Lime Street Station (SJ351905)

Access: Liverpool Lime Street is readily accessible on the local Merseyrail network, and has frequent connections on the Regional Railways and Inter City networks to most parts of the country. For details of the Merseyrail network, phone Merseytravel on 051 236 7676. For details of longer distance British Rail journeys, contact British Rail on 051 709 9696.

Liverpool lies at the Western end of the M62, and the Western end of the East Lancs Road. It is also easily accessed via the two Mersey Tunnels, reached on the Wirral side along the A41, or the M53.

There is plenty of pay and display parking in Liverpool City Centre. Alternatively, park within Kings Dock, to the south of the Albert Dock complex on the Mersey Waterfront, where the parking is free.

Ship and Mitre, Dale Street, Liverpool

The Ship and Mitre is a pleasant city-centre pub which recently won the Merseyside CAMRA pub of the year award for the range and quality of its beers. Cains Mild and Bitter are regularly available, and up to seven other real ales. Very reasonably priced meals are available every week-day lunchtime. This is a deservedly popular public house. The interior contains much wood to put you in mind of the flagship it was once named after. Fascinating stained glass vaulted ceiling and gas lamps in the interior.

The Ship and Mitre is open all day Monday to Saturday; from 11.00 am to 8.00 pm Monday and Tuesday; from 11.00 am to 11.00 pm Wednesday to Friday; and from 12.30 pm to 11.00 pm Saturday. It is closed on Sundays.

Liverpool

Liverpool is the heart of Merseyside, a brash vibrant working city which retains a unique sense of identity and humour despite the economic ills which have plagued it of late. The fine buildings within the business heart reveal the wealth which was once centred upon and generated within Liverpool. The Albert Dock complex, lovingly restored, is now one of the top tourist attractions in Britain. Here you can visit many cafes, bars and restaurants, and wander the attractive shops set among the colonnades. The Tate Gallery is situated here, and you can also visit other cultural attractions such as the Beatles Story and Animation World, with Count Duckula! The Maritime Museum rightly deserves its reputation as one of the leading museums in Britain, and presents the history of maritime Merseyside, including the economic wealth and power generated by the Slave Trade.

Birkenhead

Birkenhead lies across the River Mersey from Liverpool, and shares a former vibrant industrial heritage. The Mersey Tunnels link Birkenhead and Liverpool, but the two cities retain their own identities. Most tourists make for Liverpool, by-passing Birkenhead; this is a shame, as a little time for exploration of Birkenhead is amply rewarded, and Hamilton Square, the central Victorian focus, puts one in mind of the best architectural features of Edinburgh. John Laird, the first MP for Birkenhead, helped to shape much of the town, and references to him crop up frequently within this walk. Birkenhead Priory, the oldest building in Merseyside, dating from 1150, was established by members of the Benedictine order, and closed by order of Henry the Eighth in 1536.

The Walk

This interesting town trail takes the traveller from Liverpool Lime Street, through the historic streets of Liverpool to the newly developed Albert Dock complex. You then have the choice of a leisure cruise across the Mersey on the world famous Mersey Ferries, or alternatively you can reach Birkenhead through the Merseyrail underwater tunnel. The town trail continues through the historic heart of Birkenhead, before returning you tò Liverpool.

Alternatively, if you wish, you can split the walk into two parts, and undertake the Liverpool and Birkenhead trails on separate visits, not forgetting to take a ride on the Mersey Ferries.

1. From the main exit of Lime Street Station, turn right along Lime Street, pausing to admire the architecture and style of St George's Hall opposite. Cross over Lime Street, and pass in front of the fountain at the head of William Brown Street. Walk down this street, the only street in Liverpool without any houses, shops or offices. It houses instead the Library and the Walker Art Gallery and Museum; well worth a visit if you have time.

2. At the bottom of William Brown Street, turn right opposite the Mersey Tunnel entrance, and use the pedestrian crossing to cross the main road and turn into Dale Street, parallel to the Tunnel. You will soon pass two fine pubs, The Ship and Mitre and the Excelsior, both well worth a stop, but note that the Excelsior is closed at weekends. The Ship and Mitre serves up to nine real ales and excellent cheap food; the Excelsior sells a variety of beers from the Boddingtons stable. You will pass Hatton Garden to your right, not named after that famous son of Liverpool, Derek "Degsy" Hatton. Pass along down Dale Street, raising your eyes on both sides to admire the fine architecture, in many cases only evident above ground floor level. The fine buildings to the left are the Municipal Buildings of Liverpool City Council.

3. When you reach Castle Street to the left, Liverpool Town Hall will be to your right. Walk left along Castle Street towards Derby Square and the new Law Courts. You will pass Trials to your right, the former Law Courts.

4. At Derby Square you will find the Queens public house to the right, where you may seek suitable refreshment. The Queens is a large modern public

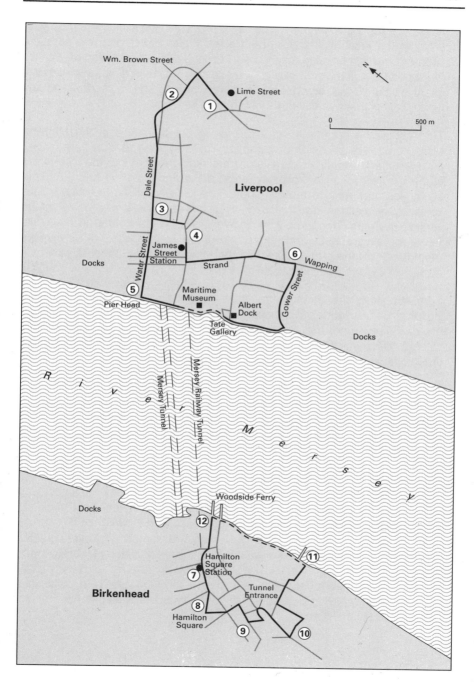

house, selling Bass beers. Meals are served at lunchtimes. Retrace your steps to the Town Hall and turn left down Water Street. You will pass the imposing building housing the Passport Office to your left. Ahead of you lies the world-famous Liver Building, with its two stone bird statues standing guard on top. Cross over Goree, and walk between the Liver Building and the equally impressive Cunard Building.

5. Turn left at the Waterfront and walk along the Mersey past the Maritime Museum and the Albert Dock complex. You may wish to stop here to visit the Maritime Museum, which gives a remarkable insight into the twin pillars of Liverpool's economic prosperity: shipbuilding and the slave trade! Alternatively, you may wish to browse in the Tate Gallery, within the Albert Dock complex, or wander around the many shops and stalls and cafes in the various pavilions. Don't forget to admire Fred's Weather Map in the dock. There are several pubs and restaurants in the Albert Dock. On leaving the Albert Dock complex, turn away from the Mersey and exit the dock either via Hartley Quay or Gower Street.

6. Turn left along the Strand, and make your way back towards the Liver Building. Before you reach it though, cross over the Strand and turn right up James Street. Enter the James Street Merseyrail Station on your left, and catch a Merseyrail electric train one stop under the river to Hamilton Square in Birkenhead.

   Alternatively you can walk back past the Liver Building to the Mersey, and catch a world famous Mersey Ferry across the river, taking in the full leisure experience. Be sure to disembark at Woodside Ferry Terminal in Birkenhead, and follow the Birkenhead part of this walk by following this sequence of paragraphs: 12, 7 to 11.

7. Emerge from Hamilton Square station, pausing to admire the wonderful red brick edifice. The station was built in 1886, when the Mersey rail tunnel was built to run in competition with the ferries. The rail tunnel was originally steam-operated, and therefore dirty and unpopular. Following conversion to electric operation in 1903, the rail tunnel assumed an ever greater importance in relation to the slower ferry network. The tall red brick tower originally housed the hydraulic system to power the lifts to convey passengers to the platforms, 100 feet below the surface. Turn right into Hamilton Street, having paused to admire the view back across the Mersey towards the Liver Buildings.

8. After 100 yards you will reach Hamilton Square. Take time to explore this attractive Victorian square fully. The buildings are constructed of local sandstone, and the roofs were originally made of Welsh slate. Walk to the middle of the square, where you will find a memorial to Queen Victoria. You will also have a fine view of Birkenhead Town Hall, constructed in 1882, and the War Memorial in front dating from 1925. You will also find a statue of John Laird, the first MP for Birkenhead, if you examine the west facing aspect of Hamilton square. Return to Hamilton Street, and turn first left past the Town Hall into Duncan Street. Then turn first right into Albion Street, where you will find the attractive Barristers public house, a comfortable town pub serving Cains, Higsons and Boddingtons beers.

9. On leaving the Barristers, proceed forwards, and turn diagonally left into Cross Street, running along the facade of a parade of shops dating from 1847. You will see the mouth of Kingsway Tunnel, built in 1837, ahead of you. Bear round the apex of the shopping precinct triangle, and cross Chester Street at the pedestrian crossing. Turn right and continue to walk along Chester Road in the direction of the Tunnel entrance.

10. Take the first turning on the left, signposted to the Priory, and walk towards Birkenhead Priory, the oldest building on Merseyside. The Priory is well worth a visit and is open Tuesday through Sunday, but note that on Sunday it is only open in the afternoon. The remains of the church of St Mary lie to the rear of the Priory, and you can spot the tombstone of John Laird, first MP of Birkenhead, in the graveyard between the two buildings. On leaving the Priory, turn right and walk down Priory Street, turning right into Ivy Street at the junction. To your right you will see the remains of Cammell Laird shipyards, a famous part of Birkenhead's prosperity founded on shipbuilding. This yard closed in 1993; a sad result of short-sighted economic and industrial policies! Cross over Church Street and walk down to the waterfront at Monks Ferry.

11. Use the new pedestrian walkway to walk leftwards along the river front to Woodside ferry terminal. You can enjoy splendid views across the Mersey towards the Anglican and Metropolitan Cathedrals, the Albert Dock complex, and the Liver and Cunard Buildings at Pier Head. On reaching the ferry terminal, you may pause a while to refresh yourself in the attractive cafe. If you are returning to Liverpool by ferry, this is your departure point.

12. From the ferry terminal, bear to the right of the new Woodside bus station.

Have a look at the tram tracks in situ: this is the site of the first street railway, opened in 1860, originally powered by horses, and later converted to electric tramway operation. Walk past the Dock Gates, with the Watchman's Hut in the middle, and you will reach the Shore Road Pumping Station, the Giant Grasshopper, on your right. This pumping station was opened in 1885 to keep water out of the Mersey rail tunnel. It is still in operation, and is open to visitors Tuesday through Sunday:. note that on Sundays it is only open in the afternoon. Cross Canning Street and walk past the attractively restored Pier Hotel, originally opened in 1860. Beyond it lies the stone building, now Good Food Fayre, which was originally the first chemist's shop in Birkenhead. Fifty yards further on you will come to Hamilton Square station, where you can catch a train back under the Mersey to Liverpool.

The Pier

18. HALE

Route: Hale – Hale Head – Mersey Way – Hale

Distance: 3 miles

Map: OS Pathfinder 739 (1:25000) Runcorn and Widnes

Start: Childe of Hale, Hale (SJ469823)

Access: Hale lies 3 miles south-west of Widnes; just east of Liverpool Speke Airport and 1.5 miles south of the A562.

Car parking is available on street round the village green; off street parking is available at the recreation ground/park just to the west of the Childe of Hale public house.

The village bus stop is also sited on the village green (Church End); for details of bus services contact Cheshire Bus on Chester 602666.

Childe of Hale, Hale (051 425 2954)

The Childe of Hale is a comfortably furnished large three-roomed inn with a small beer garden and children's play area outside. Food is available Monday to Friday lunchtimes 12.00 noon to 2.30 pm. Hand-pumped ales from Cains and Higsons are available.

The Childe of Hale is open all day Monday to Saturday 12.00 noon to 11.00 pm; on Sunday normal opening hours apply.

Hale

Hale is an attractive rural village of thatched and whitewashed cottages surrounded by industrial developments and Speke Airport. Despite its proximity to industry, it manages to preserve a tranquil air. Its major claim to fame is the grave of John Middleton, the "Childe of Hale". In 1617 this son of Hale, reputed to be over 9 feet in height, was taken to

the court of King James I. He soon fell out with the King and was forced
to take early retirement.

The Childe of Hale

The Walk

1. Having paused to admire the cottages to the left of the village store and post office, turn right (east) from the Childe of Hale and walk down Church Lane. You will pass some beautiful thatched cottages.

2. Turn left down Within Way, situated just beyond a fine ornate red brick house. Follow this attractive country lane as it leads you down to the River Mersey. Industrial views open up in front of you and to the left; the Runcorn Bridge is a dominating sight. Agricultural and rural aspects prevail to your right. The lane bends to the right and then to the left. Pass through the stile and straight on; this is signposted to Lighthouse Way.

3. Pass through the next stile just before the Mersey, and turn right to follow

the Mersey Way. A church can be seen across the river on the waterfront; presumably this serves the dockers! A variety of birds can be espied in the grass and mudflats to your left. The lighthouse at Hale Head soon comes into view: continue to walk towards this. Work was carried out on the River Mersey here to improve communication between Liverpool and the Bridgewater Canal at Runcorn. The channel was marked with navigation buoys in 1783; in 1836 the first lighthouse was constructed on this site. The present lighthouse dates from 1906, and was in use until 1958. The Clwydian mountains can be seen across the river on a clear day from this viewpoint. People have attempted to ford the river here, with varying degrees of success. The authors strongly advise against attempting this!

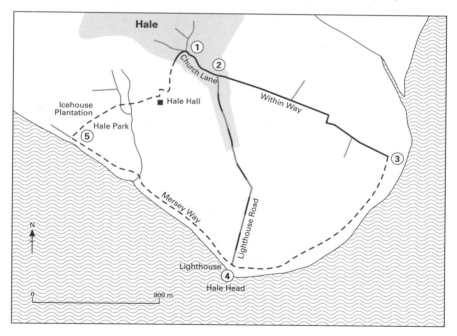

4. Turning right along Lighthouse Road from Hale Head will return you after a mile to the centre of Hale, passing the Parish church of St Mary on the way; a church was first constructed on this site as long ago as 1081, being rebuilt in 1758 and 1977. We suggest, however, that you continue straight ahead along the Mersey Way to enjoy the views and wildlife. You will soon pass over a wooden bridge. Continue walking for a further 500 yards until you

reach a stile, at the point where a plantation of trees, Icehouse Plantation, joins from the right. You can walk down the steps to the shoreline at this point if you wish; otherwise you should turn round and retrace your steps to the lighthouse, Lighthouse Road, and the village of Hale.

5. Alternatively, pass the stile and turn right along the well-beaten track which leads you through the plantation. This is not an official footpath, but as the ground testifies it is a path used extensively by locals. Bear with the path through the trees; when you cross a farm track, the path continues ahead and slightly to the left. Pass through a wooden stile and Hale Hall appears to your right. Take the driveway to the left and pass through the park and recreation ground, returning to the village green, and turning right to enjoy a fine pint of Cains or Higsons at the Childe of Hale.

19. PERCH ROCK

Route: New Brighton Railway Station – Perch Rock – Vale Park – Magazine Brow – New Brighton Railway Station

Distance: 3 miles

Map: OS Pathfinder 721 (1:25000) Wallasey

Liverpool A-Z Street Atlas (page 42)

Start: New Brighton Railway Station (SJ304939)

Access: New Brighton is served by the Merseyrail electric services. For details of trains contact Merseytravel on 051 236 7676.

New Brighton lies 2 miles north-east of Junction 1 of the M53 along the A544, just over the Mersey estuary from central Liverpool.

Car parking is possible on-street along Victoria Road, and there is also plenty of parking space along Kings Parade.

The Magazine, Magazine Brow, New Brighton (051 639 6055)

This is a quaint, traditional pub with lots of character and lots of horse brasses and timber. There are many rooms and a beer garden in which to enjoy an excellent pint of Bass. Food is served at lunchtimes (Monday to Friday 12.00 noon – 2.00 pm). The Magazine overlooks New Brighton Promenade, and is in a very attractive residential area close to Vale Park. The Magazine is full of atmosphere and opens all day Monday to Saturday (11.00 am – 11.00 pm); normal Sunday hours apply.

New Brighton

New Brighton is a pleasant, traditional and underrated seaside resort. It cannot be said that it has enjoyed better days, because it never has enjoyed a true heyday. This is a great pity because the resort has much to offer: an attractive setting, beautiful safe sands, parks, Promenades, and attractive pubs. It also once claimed the tallest structure in Europe: the New Brighton Tower. This was built between 1896 and 1900, and at 173m was some 15m higher than the earlier constructed Blackpool Tower. It was lit by 20,000 light bulbs, and was described by one awestruck observer as "a dazzling newcomer to the Wonders of the World". It fell into disuse during the First World War, and was demolished between 1919 and 1920.

Perch Rock Lighthouse

The Walk

1. From the main entrance of the railway station turn right up Atherton Street, and immediately left along Victoria Road. This road leads you down to the remains of New Brighton Pier, which has gone the way of many of England's piers.

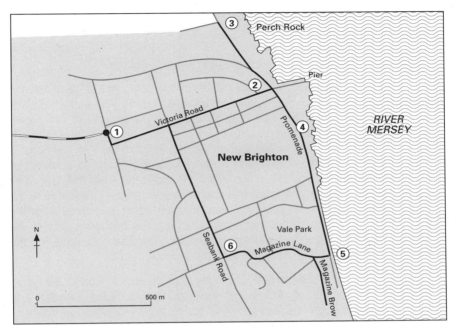

2. Turn left at the bottom of Victoria Road, and stroll past the Floral Pavilion. You can see the docks at Bootle over the Mersey estuary to your right. Cross over the road and make for Fort Perch Rock on Perch Rock, taking care to admire the pastel shades of the Palace to your left. Fort Perch Rock was built to guard the entrance to the Port of Liverpool: it may be visited at certain times, for details contact the Tourist Information Office in the Floral Pavilion.

3. At low tide you can walk around the Fort, and approach the Perch Rock lighthouse. Make your way back to the remains of the Pier. There are excellent views to the left from the Pier over the estuary towards central Liverpool. You can make out the twin-towered Liver Building, also the distinctive shapes of the two cathedrals. Walk past the pier along the pedestrian way and skirt Tower Gardens; formerly the 35 acres of rolling woodland belonged to the short-lived New Brighton Tower (see above).

4. Continue to walk along the Promenade, which now becomes Magazine Promenade. The attractive Vale Park, opened in 1899, runs along to the right of the Promenade. This area derives its name from the fact that it

became the Powder Magazine for the Port of Liverpool in 1750, relocated from the other side of the Mersey for greater safety, though not necessarily for the greater safety of the residents of New Brighton! Ships deposited all their gunpowder here before entering the Port of Liverpool.

5. At the end of Vale Park, turn right up Magazine Lane, immediately beyond the public shelter on your right, and before reaching the War Memorial. Turn down Magazine Brow, the first road to the left. The house on the corner here is Battery House, formerly the Liscard Battery, dating from 1854, and built to back up Fort Perch Rock in preventing entry to the Mersey Estuary and the Port of Liverpool by enemy ships. A couple of hundred yards along Magazine Brow you will reach first the Pilot Boat and then the Magazine public houses. Pause here to refresh yourself. Now retrace your steps to the corner of Magazine Brow and Lane, and turn left uphill, and away from the Promenade. Pass the Round House on your left: this is the remains of the hut used by the Magazine's watchmen to keep a look-out on shipping in the Mersey. Continue up Magazine Lane to the brow of the hill.

6. Turn right here at the parade of shops into Seabank Road; this soon becomes Rowson Street. At the junction with Victoria Road, turn left and retrace your steps to the station.

The Magazine

20. NEW BRIGHTON

Route: New Brighton – Mockbeggar Wharf – New Brighton

Distance: 5 miles

Map: OS Pathfinder 721 (1:25000) Wallasey; Liverpool A-Z Street Atlas

Start: New Brighton Railway Station (SJ304939)

Access: Direct access by rail from Liverpool: contact Merseytravel for information on 051 236 7676. Access by road from Liverpool is via Mersey Tunnels, and then follow signs for New Brighton Promenade. If arriving by car there is ample parking space on the promenade.

Royal Victoria Hotel, New Brighton (051 691 1309)

The Royal Victoria is a large hotel in an elevated position overlooking the railway, and with splendid views across the estuary. Its large front bar has massive windows which ensure a clear view even if you can't get a window seat. The bar is very comfortable, and sofas complete with coffee tables lend a genteel air to the proceedings. The rear bar offers snooker tables and there are also seats outside, with the same wonderful views as obtained in the front bar.

Real ales on offer from the long wooden bar are John Smiths Bitter, Ruddles County and Websters Yorkshire Bitter. Food is available between 12.00 noon and 9.00 pm. The pub is open all day Monday to Saturday (11.00 am to 11.00 pm); normal Sunday hours apply.

New Brighton

A seaside town at the mouth of the Mersey, which displays the same fascination with golf as the rest of the Wirral. For further details of New Brighton, see the introduction to Walk No. 19.

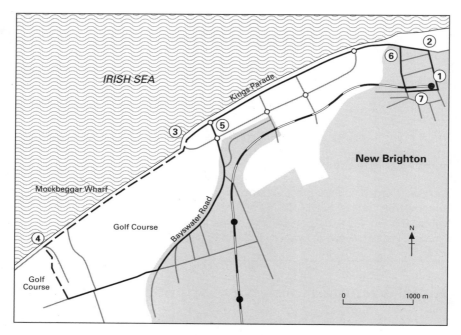

The Walk

1. On leaving New Brighton Railway Station, through the main exit, turn left onto Atherton Street and proceed down towards the Promenade. Notice the way in which number 28 appears to be part of a continuous wall rather than an individual house.

2. At the bottom of the road, cross the road between you and the sea and then turn left along Kings Parade. Bear to the right of a small lake used for model boats and continue along Kings Parade, atop the sea wall. Once past the slipways, the pavement beneath your feet turns to pink, so just follow the colour as it continues beside the sea. The small rock outcrops to your left at the base of the hill, are known as the noses.

3. About half a mile along the Promenade, there is a large triangle of groynes forming another defence against the tides. Continue along Coastal Drive, or along the wide pale sands.

4. After another half mile or so, just before a slipway and car park, turn left onto a signed bridleway. This bridleway forms a narrow road, running through the dunes to the right of the golf course. At the end of this bridleway turn left at the T-junction along a tree- and hedge-lined lane. The golf links are now to your left. On reaching the end of this lane, turn left onto the main road. Walk along Bayswater Road past the entrance to Wallasey Golf Club and the solid looking edifice of the church of St Nicholas. The sea soon comes into view again.

5. Once back on the Promenade, turn right and retrace your steps along it.

6. This time, turn right up Portland Street, which is steep. However, the Royal Victoria Hotel can be seen ahead, to encourage any falterers. This provides an opportunity for rest and refreshment.

7. On leaving the pub turn right along Victoria Street and then immediately left onto Atherton Street and the railway station for your journey home.

Hotel Victoria

21. WEST KIRBY

Route: West Kirby – Hoylake – Hilbre Point – West Kirby

Distance: 4.5 miles

Map: OS Pathfinder 738 (1:25000) Heswall, Birkenhead and Liverpool (South)

Start: West Kirby Rail Station (SJ213868)

Access: West Kirby can be accessed by rail or bus from Merseyside, or by car on the M53. There is ample car parking space in West Kirby; the car park in Dee Road by the Safeway car park is the most convenient one for this walk.

The Dee Hotel, West Kirby (051 625 8541)

The Dee is a large hotel opposite West Kirby rail station, and recently modernised. There is a huge lounge bar, very comfortable and quiet at lunch time. The beers are Tetleys Mild and Bitter. The Dee Hotel is open all day (11.30 am to 11.00 pm) Monday to Saturday; normal Sunday opening hours apply. There is an outdoor area at the rear.

The Plasterers Arms, Hoylake (051 632 3023)

A small traditional local on a quiet back street in Hoylake. A cosy bar at the front and a larger back room with dart board, there are also a few seats outside for sunny days and a beer garden at the rear. The beers available are Flowers IPA, Flowers Original, Fremlins, Hartleys XB, Castle Eden and a guest beer. Snacks and filled rolls are available at all times. This is a very pleasant, quiet pub – no juke box or canned music – in which to enjoy a good pint. Families are welcomed, and there is a playground opposite the pub.

The Plasterers Arms is open all day (11.30 am to 11.00 pm) Monday to Saturday; on Sunday normal hours apply. The building is at least 200 years old, and there is a mini "museum" behind the bar containing such gems as "a jar of pickled people".

The Plasterers' Arms

West Kirby

A pleasant sea-side town, with a beautiful mile long sandy beach complete with horse rides and wonderful views across the Dee estuary. Hilbre Island Local Nature Reserve is accessed from West Kirby, entrance is free of charge but permits are required in advance. Access on foot is restricted by tides which cut off the islands for up to six hours, twice a day. Hilbre Island housed a religious community, until the dissolution of the monasteries.

Hoylake

Home of the Royal Liverpool Golf Course. The beach is beautiful sand and dunes. Hoylake's development was, like that of West Kirby, linked to progress in transport; by 1888 it had a direct rail link to Liverpool. However, hotel developments date from 1792. Most of the buildings date from the 19th century and the coming of the railway.

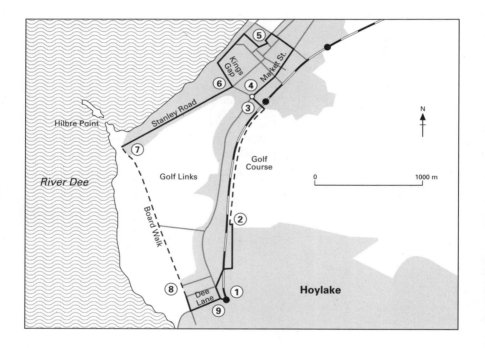

The Walk

1. From West Kirby rail station turn right along Grange Road, after about 50 yards turn right down Bridge Road which carries you over the railway line. Once across the bridge turn left down Orrysdale Road, which mutates into Anglesey Road as it passes the primary school.

2. The road curves to the right, but we take the footpath signed "Public Footpath to Hoylake", which bears left, then straightens up to follow the railway line. A glance back to the right reveals the war memorial on Grange Hill. The path is soon skirting the edge of Hoylake Golf Course to your right, while the railway continues to your left.

3. After about three quarters of a mile, turn left into Carr Lane, crossing the railway line in front of Hoylake Station, a wonderful 1930s style edifice.

4. At the roundabout turn right onto Market Street, and continue past shops and St Luke's Methodist church. On reaching Trinity Road, turn left into it and continue until you reach Back Sea View. Turn left into Back Sea View which with a left turn brings you to The Plasterers Arms and a chance for an excellent pint in peaceful surroundings.

5. On leaving the Plasterers Arms, go straight on from the pub door, then turn right down Government Road which brings you down to the sea front. Turn left along the promenade in front of the lifeboat station. After a short stretch the sea front road ends and the houses and gardens go right down to the beach, at this point turn left along the road named Kings Gap. Note the old lighthouse to your left, the survivor of a pair, now part of a private house.

(Alternatively, you could continue along the beach, although this will depend on the tide and weather conditions).

6. Turn right at the Green Lodge Hotel and continue along Stanley Road. Alternatively you might be tempted to stop for a pint of Burtonwood at this large hostelry with extensive beer garden. As you walk along the road the buildings on the left give way to the Royal Liverpool Golf Course. The view is splendid, with the Welsh hills rising in the background across the Dee estuary, but the Royal Hotel, constructed in 1792 by Sir John Stanley, is, sadly, no longer standing. There are some fascinating houses along this road in a bewildering variety of styles, note especially towards the end of the road the lighthouse attached to a newly-built house.

7. At the end of the road, a jetty descends to the sea. Hilbre Island is straight ahead (note that is unsafe to attempt to walk to the island from this point, information on safe routes and tide tables are available at West Kirby). Turn left at the jetty and follow the path along the rocks. On rounding the corner from the jetty bear left into the dunes in front of the last house. A path soon

becomes clear leading to a board-walk, which leads you between the Royal Liverpool Golf Club to the left and the Red Rocks Marsh Nature Reserve to your right.

The board-walk undulates with the pattern of the dunes, watch out for the odd broken board. The three islands of Hilbre, Middle Eye or Little Hilbre and Little Eye can be clearly seen, and again the Welsh hills are in the background. A variety of animal and plant life may be seen, more than two hundred types of birds have been spotted along this route. The nature reserve is also home to the rare natterjack toad.

The board-walk becomes a sandy path through the dunes, then returns as steps to the left up to an elevated view point. West Kirby and the golf course lie to the left, the three islands and Wales to the right.

(An alternative to the board-walk is simply to follow the beach to West Kirby.)

8. The board-walk ends in steps down to the beach at West Kirby. Follow the beach for a short while then up onto South Parade. Turn left at the Wirral Sailing Club into Dee Lane.

If you wish to visit Hilbre Island details of safe routes and tide timings are available at the West Kirby slipway.

9. At the end of Dee Lane turn right into Grange Road, the station is ahead of you, but why not visit the Dee Hotel, opposite the station, for a pint of Tetleys while awaiting your train?

22. HESWALL

Route: West Kirby – Wirral Way – Thurstaston – Lower Heswall – Heswall

Distance: 6.5 miles

Map: OS Pathfinder 738 (1:25000) Heswall, Birkenhead and Liverpool (South)

Start: West Kirby Rail Station (SJ213868)

Access: West Kirby can be accessed mostly easily by public transport by using the Merseyrail electric services. West Kirby station lies close to Dee Road, the start point for this linear walk to Heswall, which requires a return to West Kirby by bus. For details of Merseyrail electric services contact Merseytravel on 051 236 7676; similarly contact the same number for details of the regular bus services for the return journey from Heswall bus station.

West Kirby lies 4 miles west of the M53, and is best approached by leaving the Motorway at Junction 2. A public car park is next to the Safeway car park along Dee Road, at the beginning of the walk.

Dee View Inn, Dee View Road, Lower Heswall (051 342 2320)

This pleasant pub lies on a hairpin bend overlooking Lower Heswall, the Dee Estuary and the Welsh hills. It serves fine beers from Thwaites, Boddingtons and Whitbread, and good, simple and substantial fare is available at lunchtimes. The Dee View Inn is open all day (12.00 noon to 11.00 pm) Monday to Saturday; normal Sunday hours apply. Children over 12 years old are welcomed.

Thurstaston

Thurstaston is a pleasant rural village situated just north of the Wirral Way. The village centre, mainly comprised of fine red Cheshire sandstone buildings, includes the fine church of St Bartholomew. Thurstaston Common lies to the north, on the other side of the A540.

Heswall

Heswall is very much a retirement and commuter-belt community, comprising some of the most affluent areas of Merseyside. It is a straggling community, threaded through by footpaths, some of them very attractive.

Coping with a stile near Heswall

Wirral Way

The Wirral Way is a linear country park formed along the route of the former Parkgate, Chester and Birkenhead Junction Railway. The first section of the line from Hooton to Parkgate was opened in 1866, and twenty years later it was extended northwards to West Kirby, linking in with the Wirral Railway. Original plans to extend into North Wales were dropped. The line was intended to serve Neston Colliery, but it was also extensively used by local farmers and merchants for the transport of produce and goods. Tourists and trippers used the railway for access to the seaside at Parkgate and West Kirby. However, competition from the diesel bus and the motor car proved too tough: the line was closed to passengers in 1956, and the track was lifted when goods workings ceased in 1962. The Wirral Way now provides an attractive green corridor for leisure activities.

The Walk

1. From West Kirby station turn left into Dee Lane, and walk past the public car park, which is by the Safeway car park. At the Wirral Sailing Club, turn left and either walk along South Parade, or preferably turn right and walk around the Marine Lake along the pleasant causeway which appears from the mainland to disappear below the water-line; this path cannot be used at high tide!

2. At the end of the Marine Lake turn left with the road past West Kirby Sailing Club, and then pass straight ahead along Sandy Lane. Pass Hilbre Road to the left, and Macdona Drive to the right.

3. Cross an old railway bridge and then turn immediately right and find the signposted gap in the fence at the corner of Yorke Avenue which leads you down some steep steps to the Wirral Way. Turn left along Wirral Way.

   Continue walking along the Wirral Way for about 1.5 miles; the path is generally enclosed by foliage, but at times views open out to your right over the estuary. Continue successively past Cubbins Green, a picnic area to your left, and a golf links to your right. Keep to the neater of the two tracks, which is often gravelled; the other muddier track is for bikes and horses. At intervals you will need to cross roads, where the bridges have disappeared. Beautiful purple roses line the track in places in Summer. Pass under Simon's Bridge, and then under Links Bridge. You will pass a caravan site to your right.

4. When you reach the site of an old station, marked by the overgrown platform to your right, pass up to the left before the car park and walk up to the main road. Turn right here along Station Road, and walk towards the

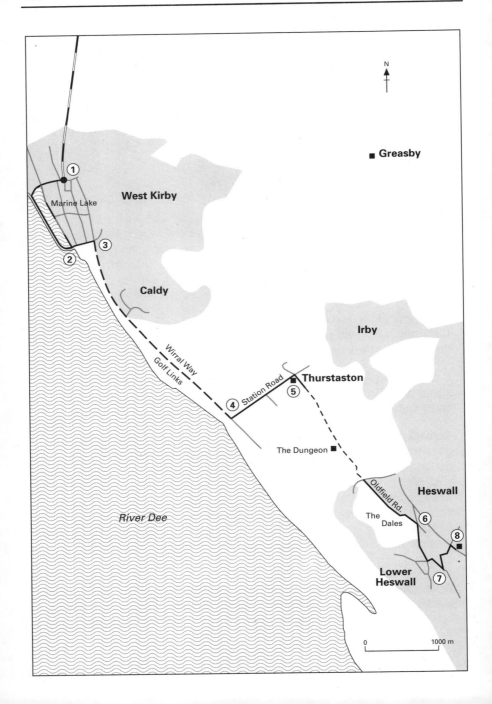

village of Thurstaston which is in the distance, marked by the church spire of St Bartholomew. On reaching the village bear right with the road towards the church. St Bartholomew was rebuilt in 1885 in red sandstone: the imposing tower belies a small interior, a juxtaposition commented on with approval by Pevsner.

5. Ignore the road to the left at the junction, and pass on to the left of the church along Church Lane. Your footpath to Heswall is signposted straight ahead, beyond a red brick archway to the right. The footpath passes straight on and over a stile to the left of a metal gate. This is a truly gorgeous path which takes the crest of the hill, and affords really amazing views. Pass over several stiles, and look out for the Dungeon, a sunken pool to your right. Go straight ahead through a further succession of stiles. The path bends 90 degrees to the right, and then to the left and over a red stone stile. Cross over the farm track and continue straight on, keeping all the farm buildings to your right. The path eventually becomes a road: keep straight on along Oldfield Road until the end.

6. At the end of Oldfield Road, turn right downhill along Thurstaston Road. At the junction turn left up Dee View Road, and bear with the road as it bends rightwards. The Dee View Hotel lies on the left at the end of the road, on the crest of the hill, and lives up to its name.

7. On leaving the pub, turn left up the Mount, and bear right with the road as it brings you to Telegraph Road, the Heswall main drag. Turn right along Telegraph Road.

8. Heswall bus station lies 200 yards along the road on the left. You can catch your return bus to West Kirby from here. The return journey lasts about 30 minutes. (For details of bus services contact Merseytravel on 051 236 7676).

23. FRANKBY

Route: Frankby – Harrock Wood – Irby – Thurstaston – Frankby

Distance: 5 miles

Map: OS Pathfinder 738 (1:25000) Heswall Birkenhead and Liverpool (South)

Start: Frankby Village Green, by Frankby Post Office (SJ245868)

Access: Frankby is accessible by bus from Heswall, Birkenhead and Liverpool. Contact Merseytravel on 051 236 7676 for details of buses. Bus stops are sited at Frankby Village Green.

Frankby lies on the B5239, 3 miles west of Birkenhead, 2 miles east of Hoylake. Frankby Village Green lies just east of the junction between the B5139 and the B5140. Limited parking is available around the green.

Irby Mill, Irby Mill Hill (051 604 0194)

This attractive sandstone country pub, formerly a mill outbuilding, lies one mile north of Irby. The pleasant interior contains a lounge and public bar. Meals are served lunchtimes and evenings. There is an outside drinking area, where children are welcome. When the authors visited a wide range of real ales was available, including Boddingtons, Cains Mild and Bitter, Jennings Bitter, Tetleys and Theakstons. The landlord also operates a guest beer policy.

The Irby Mill is open 11.30 am to 3.00 pm and 5.00 pm to 11.00 pm Monday to Friday; it is open all day (11.30 am to 11.00 pm) on Saturdays; on Sundays normal opening hours apply. Food is available 12.00 noon to 2.00 pm Monday to Saturday.

Farmers Arms, Hillbark Road, Frankby (051 677 5129)

This pleasant country pub lies opposite the vehicle entrance to Royden Hall Park. Lunchtime meals are available, and there is an extensive beer garden. There is an attractive lounge, and a marvellous old public bar, complete with darts and dominoes. The beers served are Flowers IPA, Castle Eden, and a guest beer.

The Farmers Arms is open all day (11.00 am to 11.00 pm) Monday to Saturday; normal Sunday opening hours.

The Farmer's Arms

Frankby, Irby and Thurstaston

This walk takes you through these three attractive country villages surrounded by farmland and undeveloped countryside. Thurstaston Common is a National Trust property, with red sandstone outcrops, the stone being so soft that it always seems covered in a layer of red sand. The views from Thurstaston Hill are stunning in all directions although its elevation is modest.

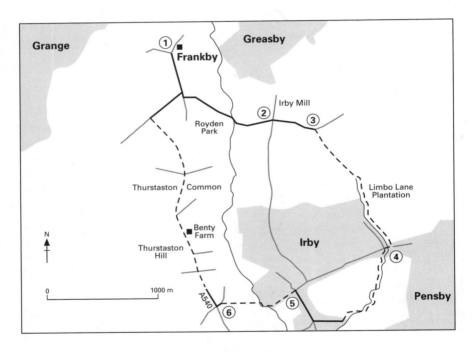

The Walk

1. Start your walk from the very attractive rural village square of Frankby. Turn left (west) from Frankby Village Green, and immediately turn south (left) at the junction with the B5140.

   After 500 yards you will reach the Farmers Arms public house: you will return to this pub later, but do drop in for a pint if you feel the urge! Note the car entrance to Royden Hall Park beyond the pub; ignore this and bear left with the road. Walk past Roodee Cottage on your right: this cottage was for sale in 1993 and the owner was offering a £50 reward for information about the culprit who was repeatedly stealing his "for sale" sign! Continue uphill with the road. There are views on your left towards the Mersey.

2. The Irby Mill public house lies at the crest of the hill, to the left of the roundabout. Pause here to admire this former mill outbuilding and perchance to sample some of the fine real ales available within. From the Irby Mill Inn continue your previous line of travel along Arrowe Brook Lane. The road gradually bends leftwards.

3. Immediately after a house on the right called Rystones, take the public footpath signposted to Irby. This is a very pleasant wide track, with hedgerows on either side which shelter much bird life. Continue onwards with the path, ignoring a stile to your left and then a path to your right. Continue along the cinder track which skirts the Limbo Lane Plantation to your left. At the end of the track turn right along the main road.

4. Cross over this road, and shortly turn left along the footpath by a stream, signposted to Pensby. This is Harrock Wood, owned by the National Trust. Cross over a wooden bridge and continue along the well-delineated path. Exit Harrock Wood via a wooden gate; cross the stream to your right by means of the concrete steps, and turn immediately left to follow the stream at the edge of the field. Continue along the left-hand field margin, keeping the stream to your left, and gradually bearing rightwards. Pass over a stile, and exit the field via a further stile. Turn right along this lane, known as Woodlands Road. When you reach the main Thurstaston Road, cross over and turn right. Just before you reach the junction at Irby Village, pause to admire Irby Hall to your left, which dates from the early 17th century, though reconstructed in 1888.

5. At the road junction, take the footpath to the left, immediately before The Anchor public house; this is signposted to Thurstaston. The path keeps to the right-hand edge of the field. At the end of the field, pass over the stile to the right by a bungalow. Pass through a concrete stile. The footpath continues ahead and to the left, behind a lamp post and to the left of the road sign for Dawlish Road. The footpath is signed here again for Thurstaston. The path may be muddy here and veers around a field with horses, first to the right and then to the left. Pass over the next stile and

walk over the field towards the buildings. Note the piles of old agricultural equipment at the top of the field. Pass over the stile at the top left of the field, and pass along the farm track towards the main road.

6. Turn left here towards the junction with the A540. Turn right at the junction, following the A540 past the Cottage Loaf pub. 300 yards past the Cottage Loaf, take the footpath to the right, signed Royden Park. This attractive path passes initially between gorse bushes, and you will see the odd mound of red Cheshire sandstone. Carry straight on, keeping a school to your right. Pass through a stile to the right of a wooden gate; do not take the path directly ahead, but the path slightly to the right by the National Trust sign, indicating that you are entering Thurstaston Common local nature reserve.

(Alternatively a brief excursion to your left here, following the appropriate signpost, will bring you to the summit of Thurstaston Hill, from where you can enjoy wonderful views of the Wirral Peninsula and surroundings.)

Thurstaston Hill

After crossing the stile at the National Trust sign the path bears downwards through a wood; pass onto the stony road and continue straight on passing Benty Farm to your right. Pass over the stile by a gate; take the right-hand path, and then immediately the left-hand fork, and descend with the path over heather-strewn common land, with fines views left to Caldy.

7. When you reach a path junction with a wall beyond, either use the stone stile over the wall, or bear left around the wall to bring you to the same position, and take the narrow pathway straight ahead between the hedgerows, to the left of the open grassy ground.

(Alternatively, stroll over the grass to the walled garden beyond, featuring a comprehensive and attractive collection of herbs and other plants. If you are lucky you may come across a beekeeping exhibition. Retrace your steps to the beginning of the narrow pathway).

Keep with the path, bearing gently to the left and keeping to the left of a car park. Cross over a driveway, and keep straight on through the bushes. Follow down a wide tree-lined path which will lead you out of Royden Park.

8. Exit Royden Park by a wooden gate, turning right along Montgomery Hill, which brings you to the Farmers Rest after 400 yards. Pause here at this fine country pub, and reward yourself with suitable refreshment. On leaving the Farmers Rest, retrace your steps northwards to Frankby Village Green.

24. PORT SUNLIGHT

Route: Bebington – Port Sunlight – Bebington

Distance: 2.5 miles

Map: Liverpool A-Z Street Atlas (page 108)

Start: Bebington Railway Station (SJ336840)

Access: Bebington lies a mile or so east of the M53; access from junction 4 along the B5137.

Bebington station is served by Merseyrail electric services from Liverpool, Birkenhead and Hooton: details from Merseytravel on 051 236 7676.

There is a car park at the station for patrons only, and on-street parking is available around the station.

Rose and Crown, Bebington (051 643 1312)

The Rose and Crown is a very good pub, serving a pleasant pint of Thwaites Mild or Bitter in the heart of the village of Bebington. Meals are served at lunchtimes (12.00 noon to 2.00 pm) Monday to Saturday, and there is a separate public bar. There are stained glass skylights to the rear of the lounge bar; attractive tiles and old photos of the area adorn the walls. The Rose and Crown was built in 1732, and enjoys a conservation order. It opens 11.30 am to 3.00 pm and 5.30 pm to 11.30 pm Monday to Thursday; Fridays and Saturdays it is open between 11.30 am and 11.00 pm; normal Sunday opening hours.

Bridge Inn, Port Sunlight (051 645 8441)

The Bridge Inn, which served Robinsons and Tetleys when the authors visited, is set in the village of Port Sunlight itself. Good bar food is served – children are welcomed – and a Les Routiers listed restaurant is attached. Food is available in the lounge every lunch (12.00 noon to 2.00 pm) and evening (6.15 pm to 8.45 pm); the restaurant is open evenings. The inn was opened in 1900 as a temperance hotel, but after being approached by villagers, Lord Leverhulme decided to put the issue of an alcoholic licence to a Port Sunlight referendum. The drinkers won, with 80% voting in favour, and the demon drink went on sale in Port Sunlight. The Famous Olde Bridge Inn is open 11.30 am to 3.00 pm and 5.00 pm to 11.00 pm Monday to Friday, 11.30 am to 11.00 pm Saturday; normal Sunday hours apply.

Port Sunlight

Port Sunlight is a garden village founded in 1888 by William Hesketh Lever, Lord Leverhulme, to house his soap factory workers. He had started 12 months previously to search for a site for industrial development and workers' housing, as his original premises on the banks of the River Mersey in Warrington had outgrown the available space. He was looking for a site close to a river to transport in the raw materials, and close to a railway line to transport out the finished products. The marshy low-lying ground which he discovered grew into the village of Port Sunlight, named after his famous Sunlight soap.

Lever believed in the need to promote the well-being of his work-force, and considered that the essential was to provide good housing with excellent local facilities: from these ideals grew the village of Port Sunlight. The building, maintenance and upkeep of the village were subsidised with part of the profits from Lever Brothers. Out of his personal wealth, Lever financed the construction of the church, the technical college and the Lady Lever Art Gallery. He also introduced many schemes for the welfare, entertainment and education of his work-force.

Lever took a great interest in planning and architecture, employing thirty different architects to design and develop the unique style of Port Sunlight; wherever you walk in the village new architectural styles assail the eye, but they do generally blend well, although it must be admitted that the village does purvey a rather artificial atmosphere, and a slightly menacing air – as in "The Prisoner".

War memorial, Port Sunlight

Port Sunlight is now designated a conservation area, and is fully contained within its original boundaries. Until recently it was necessary to be an employee or pensioner of a Unilever Company to qualify for residence in the village: the houses can now be bought on the open market. This has led to certain stresses and strains: increased house prices makes purchase more difficult for Unilever employees, while the prosperous incomers bring their own social mores, and do not take kindly to any perceived yoke, no matter how paternalistic and philanthropic. The late 20th century has caught up with Port Sunlight – this brings both advantages and disadvantages, but there is no doubt that the village retains an aura of space and quiet, a veritable oasis, though perhaps better to visit than inhabit!

The Lady Lever Art Gallery is a very fine museum: there is no entrance charge but visitors are requested to make a voluntary donation. The Gallery houses an extremely fine collection of paintings, ceramics, furniture and sculpture, mainly from the 18th and 19th centuries. Particular strong points are the pre-Raphaelite pictures, the 18th century English furniture and the Chinese ceramics. Look out in particular for the Ming Dynasty seated statue of the Goddess of Mercy, Kuan-Yin: simply superb!

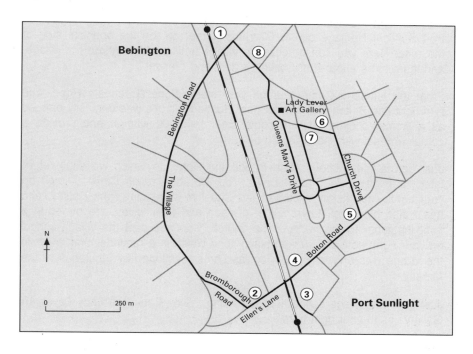

The Walk

1. From Bebington railway station turn right along Bebington Road. Pass Greendale Road to your left, and pass under the railway bridge. You will see a free car park here opposite the Oriental Delight restaurant, which can be used as an alternative to the parking arrangements described above. You will pass a beautiful large thatched cottage to your left. Of interest is the ornate clock tower attached to F R Kirk, funeral directors, to your right. You will soon reach the Rose and Crown, which lies to your left. Tarry here awhile, and savour the Thwaites, while gazing upon the stained glass skylights. Continue leftwards on leaving the pub, and then turn left down Bromborough Road. Note the attractive semi-circle of shops ahead of you in Church Road, before you turn left here.

2. Turn left again and pass down Ellens Lane. Pass under the railway bridge.

3. Turn right into Greendale Road and walk towards Port Sunlight station: this building and the wooden bus shelter on its forecourt also blend well into the Port Sunlight architectural lexicon. On reaching the station, you will see the Port Sunlight Heritage centre 50 yards further on, on the opposite side of the road. Here you can purchase a village trail, booklets about the village, and learn more about Port Sunlight's past and present.

4. From the Heritage Centre retrace your steps along Greendale Road, and turn right into Bolton Road. Walk past Hulme Hall: this was originally opened as a women's dining hall. It could cater for 2000 women and provide a complete meal with menus at 3d or 4d!

5. Just before the Famous Olde Bridge Inn Hotel, to which we shall return later, turn left down Church Drive. You will soon reach Christ Church on your right. The church is built of red Cheshire sandstone from Helsby, and has a fine pine roof. Leverhulme, his son and their wives, are buried in a tomb chamber to the north of the church. Continue past the village school on your right: note the sunken playground which is a reminder that much of the village was originally low-lying land cross-sectioned by tributaries of the Mersey.

6. Just past the village school turn left along Windy Bank: the Lady Lever Art Gallery lies to your right here.

7. Turn left again into King George's Drive just before the statue/fountain. The Diamond lies to your right, and the War Memorial ahead of you. Continue onwards, and bear up round the back of the War Memorial. This memorial, the theme of which is "defence of the home", is a very fitting tribute to the fallen of two World Wars, and a later plaque commemorates the victims of the Hillsborough disaster. From here the Famous Old Bridge Inn lies on Church Drive: pause here awhile. After suitable refreshment return to the War Memorial, and pass down Queen Mary's Drive on the other side of The Diamond.

8. Visit the Lady Lever Art Gallery, then pass the Leverhulme Memorial, erected to his memory by fellow workers, and walk down Brook Street which returns you to Bebington Station.

25. BARNSTON

Route: Heswall Railway Station – Barnston – Heswall

Distance: 3 miles

Map: OS Pathfinder 738 (1:25000) Heswall, Birkenhead and Liverpool (South)

Start: Heswall Railway Station (SJ286819)

Access: Heswall railway station is served by trains on the Wrexham to Bidston line. For service details contact British Rail on 051 709 9696. For details of connections to and from Liverpool at Bidston, contact Mersey-travel on 051 236 7676.

Heswall lies 2 miles east of the M53; access from junction 4 along the B5137. There is a car park at Heswall station for patrons only, and plenty of off-street parking in Brimstage Road by the Post Office.

Fox and Hounds, Barnston (051 648 7685)

The Fox and Hounds is an extremely pleasant village pub, a free house with no brewery tie. There are three rooms, a large lounge, a cosy bar and a small lounge off the bar where families are welcome. Tables are also available outside to the rear of the pub. The Fox and Hounds is a refreshing change in that real fires glow, while muzak and games machines have no place. The bar decor features not only the near ubiquitous horse brasses but also an unusual collection of ashtrays adorning the walls. Real ales usually available are Courage Directors' Bitter, Ruddles County and Best, Marstons Pedigree and Websters Yorkshire Bitter.

Excellent food is available daily from noon to 2.00 pm, and is deservedly popular so if you intend to eat it may be advisable to book a table in advance at peak times. The bread and butter pudding with honey, a winter special, is quite sublime!

The Fox and Hounds

The Fox and Hounds is open from 11.30 am to 3 pm and from 5.30 pm to 11 pm Mondays to Saturdays. Sunday hours are the usual 12.00 noon to 3 pm and 7 pm to 10.30 pm.

Barnston

Barnston is a small hamlet with a few working farms, a Manor House, and the excellent Fox and Hounds. The centre of the village is a conservation area, and affords a glimpse into Wirral life of times past.

The Walk

1. Leave Heswall Station car park and turn left along Brimstage Road. After 50 yards turn right along Acre Lane. At the end of the lane turn left along Barnston Road, and almost immediately right into Milner Road. Bear right at the fork into Whitefield Lane.

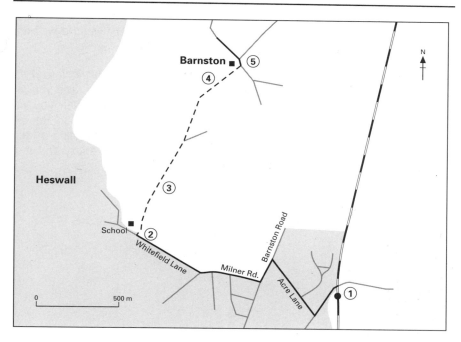

2. After about 600 yards, and just before the Whitefield junior School, take the footpath signposted to the right to Barnston. The path starts out as a narrow tree-canopied twitchell, passing over a tiny stream as it climbs a gentle gradient. Fields soon open out on both sides. Pass through a stile and follow the path along the field boundary to the left of a hedge.

3. Pass over a stile, the path now follows a route diagonally left across the field. The line of the path is visible in the grass and the next stile can be seen across the field, occupied by dairy cows. Over the next stile, across a lane, and over another stile into the next field. Again the path follows a diagonal line across the field towards some farm outbuildings and another stile. Over the stile, it may be muddy at the bottom, but there are some thoughtfully provided stepping stones. The path again follows a diagonal, this time slightly to the right along the line of a small ditch, before following the line of a hedge to your left.

4. The next stile takes you into the far end of the graveyard; note the off-cut stone, possibly from memorial stones, in the stiles; pass straight across and almost immediately out the other side. Follow the path to the right, with a

stone wall as its right-hand boundary. Keep straight on between a wall and hedge to the road.

5. The path emerges into Barnston between the church to your right, and the village Post Office to your left. Turn left past the Post Office, and you will find the Fox and Hounds just along the road on the left. When you are suitably refreshed, retrace your steps over the fields, and back to Heswall Station. If you require further refreshment in Heswall while awaiting a train, turn right along Milner Road until you reach the Sandon Arms, and then make your way back to Heswall Station.

26. EASTHAM FERRY

Route: Bromborough – Eastham Ferry – Eastham – Bromborough

Distance: 4.5 miles

Map: OS Pathfinder 738 (1:25000) Heswall Birkenhead and Liverpool (South)

Start: Bromborough Rail Station (SJ344810)

Access: Access by train from Merseyside. For those arriving by car, the station is just off the A41, there is a car park by the railway station.

Pier Bar and The Eastham Ferry Hotel, Eastham Ferry (051 327 6089)

These two buildings lie right next to the old ferry departure point. Eastham Ferry Hotel served visitors heading north or to Liverpool, who preferred to stay in a country hotel, continuing their journey by ferry. The ferry service ceased to operate in 1934.

The Pier Bar is a small comfortable bar serving Burtonwood Bitter. The walls are decorated with pictures of the area in former times. There is an outdoor drinking area. The Pier Bar is open all day Monday to Saturday (11.30 am to 11.00 pm); normal Sunday hours.

The Eastham Ferry Hotel also serves Burtonwood, and has a beer garden and family room.

Hooton Arms, Eastham Village (051 327 6783)

The Hooton Arms is a small, single room pub, made cosy by a real fire at one end, and it caters very much for the local people. Beers available are Boddingtons Bitter, Bentleys Yorkshire Bitter and Flowers IPA. Families are welcome, and there is a small patio. Food is served Monday to Saturday 11.30 am to 2.30 pm. The Hooton Arms is open all day

Monday to Saturday (11.30 am to 11.00 pm); normal Sunday hours apply.

Eastham

Eastham village is a very pretty, unexpected oasis in the midst of a series of oil terminals and storage tanks. The Eastham Ferry running across the Mersey to Liverpool, made the place very popular with travellers from the south to Liverpool. The opening of a railway between Chester and Birkenhead reduced the appeal of the ferry. Pleasure gardens were developed around the Ferry, now the Eastham Country Park, and the hotel built. Eastham Ferry was a successful resort for day outings, declining in the 1920s as individual and group mobility increased.

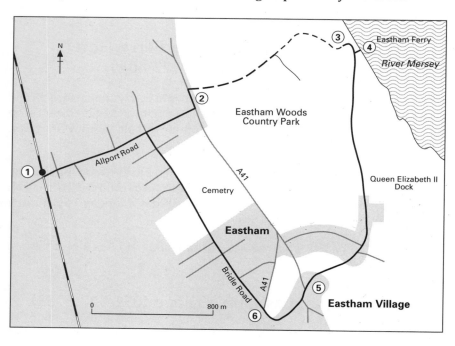

The Walk

1. If arriving by train turn left on leaving the station down Allport Road (if parked in the station car park turn right into Allport Road). Walk past a row of shops and down the tree-lined road. Straight across the first set of traffic lights and continue down Allport Road. At the next junction with traffic lights, with a Telegraph petrol station to your left and Leverhulme Sports Field ahead, cross the main road (A41) with the aid of the lights. Then turn left along the A41 for about 50 yards.

2. Turn right down a footpath signed "Eastham Country park" and "Eastham Ferry". The path is wide and tree-lined, it takes you past sports grounds offering facilities for cricket, tennis and football. Continue straight on into Eastham Woods, past a wooden gate and along the path. The path continues through attractive woodland, on one day in April the authors saw squirrels, wood anemones, a jay and a wren.

3. A car park appears on the left and some buildings ahead; turn left just before you reach the buildings, and walk down towards the Mersey. You will pass a tea garden and come to a mini-roundabout. To the left lies a picnic area overlooking the river; to continue the walk turn right at the roundabout. Almost immediately the Pier Bar comes into view on your right offering the opportunity for a pint of Burtonwood.

4. Opposite the Pier Bar lies a viewing platform with telescope; to the left you can see Liverpool, and on a clear day the cathedrals. To the right lies the entrance to the Manchester Ship Canal; ships can often be seen entering or leaving the Mersey. The construction of the Manchester Ship Canal created a marshy island in the river: a haven for birds.

To continue the walk turn right on leaving the Pier Bar and follow the road past a rather elegant red stone public toilet. This road takes you past the Eastham Ferry Hotel, also offering Burtonwood ales.

Follow the road up the hill, with the woods to your right. You will soon pass the Queen Elizabeth II Dock serving the Ship Canal. The view on the left opens up to reveal a vista of oil storage tanks. There is an interesting combination of houses, bungalows and gardens, overshadowed by the oil storage facilities. There is even a small field with a few sheep in it!

5. At the junction with a main road, The Hooton Arms is found on your right: time for a pint. On leaving the pub continue down the road past the Kingdom Hall of the Jehovahs Witnesses. Bear right at the War Memorial, passing the church of St Mary on your left. You will pass the Stanley Arms. This road takes you through the attractive old village of Eastham; bear right with the road past the Post Office.

6. At the junction with traffic lights, cross the main A41, and turn right along it, turning almost immediately left down Bridle Road. This road takes you past housing, sports fields and the Plymyard Allotments. On reaching the traffic lights controlled junction with Allport Road, turn left down Allport road to return to Bromborough railway station.

The Pier Bar, Eastham Ferry

27. PARKGATE

Route: Parkgate – Backwood Hall – Gayton – Dee Estuary – Parkgate

Distance: 4 miles

Map: OS Pathfinders 738 Heswall Birkenhead and Liverpool (South) and 756 Ellesmere Port (West) (1:25000)

Start: The Ship Hotel, The Parade, Parkgate (SJ279782)

Access: Parkgate is situated on the Dee Estuary on the B5135, close to Neston, and 1.5 miles south of the A540. On-street parking is available along the Parade, and there is a small car park off Mostyn Square.

Regular bus services link Parkgate with Chester, New Brighton, Hoylake and Liscard: contact Merseytravel on 051 236 7676 for full service details.

Neston Station lies close to Parkgate, requiring a walk of one mile along the B3135.

The Boat House, Parkgate (051 336 4187)

This attractive black and white pub, named after the ferry boats which used to ply between Parkgate and Flint across the Dee Estuary, stands at the Northern end of the Parade, close to the RSPB nature reserve. A regular ferry service operated between 1740 and 1864, when the new rail service between North Wales and Wirral took most of the trade away. The Parkgate landing place was where the Boat House now stands.

This pub is in the *Les Routiers* guide for food, and has a beer garden and children's play area. There are marvellous views across the Dee Estuary from almost every seat inside the pub, and the beer garden even has a telescope handy. Beers served are Tetleys, Theakstons Best, Greenalls Best and Thomas Greenalls Original. The Boat House is open all day Monday to Saturday (11.30 am to 11.00 pm), and food is available 12.00 noon to 2.00 pm and 6.30 to 9.30 pm. Normal pub opening hours apply on Sunday, and food is available all day.

The Boat House

The Ship Hotel (Piper's Bar), The Parade, Parkgate (051 336 3931)

This stone-fronted hotel enjoys spectacular views over the Welsh hills and Dee Estuary. The Piper's Bar, accessed from the left-hand side, serves real ales from the Oak Brewery, Websters, Cains and regular guest beers. Keenly priced bar meals are also served 12.00 noon to 2.00 pm, and 6.30 to 8.30 pm. The bar is open 11.00 am to 3.00 pm and 6.30 pm to 11.00 pm Monday to Saturday; normal Sunday opening.

Parkgate

Parkgate takes its name from its proximity to the gates of Neston Park, a deer park which has long disappeared into the mists of antiquity. Parkgate developed from being an insignificant hamlet in the 17th century to become a leading port for Ireland, as ports further up the Dee became heavily silted. It flourished in the 18th century; such diverse persons as King William III and Handel embarked here. By the 1820s it, too, became a victim of silting and the ferry trade again moved further down the river. You can still feel the atmosphere of the port while seated near the old quayside. The resort is now famed by visitors for its seafood and home-made ice cream. The facades of The Parade form a wonderful frontage facing the magnificent Dee Estuary with its salt marshes and flats.

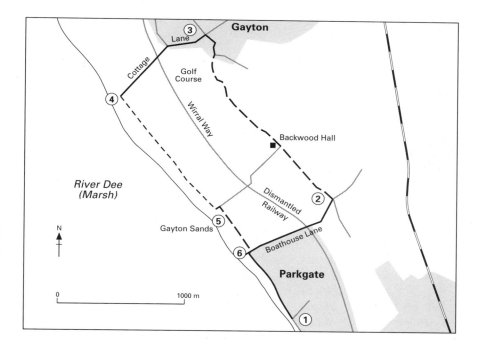

The Walk

1. Your walk starts facing the Ship Hotel on the Parade. The fine black and white building to the right is Mostyn House School, a private day school for children aged 4 to 18. Walk northwards along the Parade, admiring the views over the marshes and salt flats of the Dee Estuary towards the Welsh hills. Just beyond the Ship Hotel lies Nichols ice cream store; the fine home-made ice creams sold in this store since 1937 have won 23 national

prizes: try them! Walk past Mostyn Square, and you can admire the Old Watch House jutting into the Parade: this house was used as a look out for customs officers for many years in their bid to curb the regular smuggling which took place over the Dee. Goods seized by customs officers included brandy, rum, gin, starch, cotton, hair powder and soap!

On reaching the Boat House public house at the end of the Parade, turn right along Boat House Lane. You will be able to return to the Boat House later. Cross over the former rail bridge which straddles the Wirral Way. Continue along the road for a further 400 yards as it bears upwards and leftwards.

2. Take the footpath to the left opposite Wood Lane. Continue straight along this track, and when you reach the buildings, keep the farm buildings to your right and Backwood Hall to your left. Pass through the white wooden gate to the right of the path and continue onwards to cross a stile over the stream which marks the Cheshire and Merseyside boundary. Pass straight on towards the metal gate, and take the stile to the left by the decrepit wooden gate. This now takes you along the right hand edge of Heswall golf course: the 16th tee, a par 3 hole of 151 yards, lies to your left. Continue to walk along the right-hand edge of the golf course, ignoring the alternative route signed to the right.

By the wooden gating and stone steps to the right, take the path straight ahead and right, signposted Gayton, which leads through attractive hedgerows. Pass through a stile and continue straight on; the path bears upwards. On reaching the crest of the hill, take the second turning on the left – the lane is cobbled – passing The Old Farm, the first building on your left. Emerge from Gayton Farm Road, and pause to admire the fine red Cheshire sandstone outcrop across the road.

3. Turn left and walk down Cottage Lane, passing the entrance to Heswall Golf Club. Cross over the Wirral Way again, and continue your descent towards the Dee. At the bottom the very attractive Gayton Cottage lies to your right, and the Dee Estuary stretches out in front of you again.

4. Take the steps to your left and walk along the wall composed of red Cheshire sandstone blocks. You can enjoy fine views in all directions: The Club House and golf course to the left, Parkgate Parade ahead of you, and Flint over the estuary in Wales. After 3/4 of a mile, and on nearing Parkgate, bear leftwards with the path away from the Dee and pass through the stile.

5. In the Old Baths Car Park to your right stands an information board erected by the Royal Society for the Protection of Birds (RSPB), which owns and administers this stretch of the Dee Estuary known as Gayton Sands Nature Reserve. You can enjoy excellent views over the estuary from here, the RSPB reserve comprising 5040 hectares of salt marshes. This is a rich feeding ground and safe roosting area for one of the largest number of ducks and wading birds wintering in the British Isles. Birds to be seen include shelduck and teal in Autumn and Winter; oystercatchers, plovers and curlews during the high Spring tides; and short-eared owls and peregrines in the Winter.

6. Resume the track until you reach the Boat House on the corner. You can refresh yourself here and still enjoy the fine estuarial views. From the Boat House retrace your steps along the Parade towards the Ship Hotel, not forgetting to sample the ice cream. Why not take some potted shrimps home for tea? Relax in the Piper's Bar of the Ship Hotel with a well-deserved drink.

28. RABY

Route: Willaston – Raby – Willaston

Distance: 4.5 miles

Map: OS Pathfinder 756 (1:25000) Ellesmere Port (West)

Start: Village Green, Willaston (SJ330776)

Access: Willaston is situated on the B5133, 3 miles east of Neston, 2 miles west of Hooton, straddling the county boundary between Cheshire and Merseyside. Parking is available around the village square.

Regular bus services link Willaston with Neston, Hooton Station, Chester and Ellesmere Port; contact Cheshire Bus on Chester 602666 for full service details.

Pollard Inn, Willaston (051 327 4615)

The Pollard Inn is an attractive old sandstone pub and hotel, well tucked away behind the village green in Willaston. Cains Bitter, Stones and Greenalls Original were the real ales on pump at the authors' visit. Lunchtime bar snacks (Monday to Friday 12.00 noon to 2.30 pm, and 12.00 noon to 1.30 pm Saturday) and Sunday roasts are available, and in addition there is a full restaurant service. There are many tables in the large grassed garden, and a children's play area. There is also a glass conservatory attached to the bar area. Opening hours are 11.30 am to 11.00 pm Monday to Saturday, with normal Sunday opening. A cannon ball was recently found embedded in one of the walls, presumably fired during the Civil War.

Raby

Raby is a tiny, quiet agricultural community: the arrival of the milk tanker or the brewer's wagon at the Wheatsheaf Inn are big events here. The thatched roof of the Wheatsheaf Inn dating from 1611 is the focal point.

Willaston

Willaston is a smart Cheshire village handily sited for walks along the Wirral Country Way. The attractive village green is dominated by a large copper beech tree. Among the interesting buildings surrounding the green are the Old Red Lion, a former public house, and the black and white Memorial Hall.

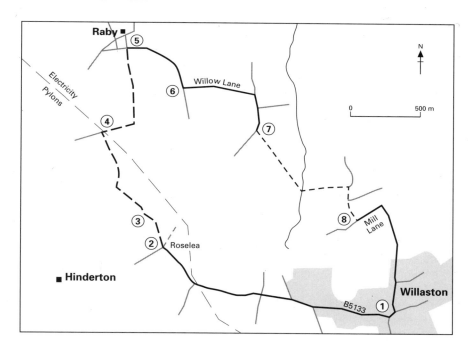

The Walk

1. With your back to the village green, turn left along the B5133. Pass the village shops, and Christ Church on your right. Go past Birkenhead Road, Lydiate Lane and Two Oaks Farm, all to your right. Pass Banks Hill Road to your left, and walk straight ahead along Quarry Road by a pylon. There is an attractive old tower across the field to your left.

2. Immediately past Roselea there are two footpaths to your right; ignore the track that continues straight on past Rose House, turning left instead opposite Rose House and passing through a rusty metal gate to follow a path along the right-hand edge of a field.

3. Just before the end of the field, take the stile to your right and pass down and through a small wood. The path bears left and then straightens. This is a very well-defined path. At the right time of year the path is lined with bluebells, and a variety of butterflies can be spotted.

4. On emerging from the wood, turn right along a grassy path. After 400 yards, turn left with the path which now becomes a grassy lane and leads you towards Raby.

5. When the lane ends, the Wheatsheaf Inn lies 50 yards straight ahead of you on the right-hand side of the road. The Wheatsheaf is a beautiful unspoilt village inn. It has a thatched roof, and marvellous wooden bar fittings and furniture. A wide array of real ales and malt whiskies is available. There are some benches to the front of the pub. It is a genuine delight to drink in this tranquil setting! On leaving the Wheatsheaf walk back along The Green to the junction, and turn left (east).

6. After 400 yards take the road to your left, Willow Lane, opposite a white house. Pass a fisherman's pond to your right, and when you reach the next road junction turn right. Ignore Benty Heath Lane to your left.

7. Just round a bend in the road take the public bridleway to your left signposted to Willaston: this is an attractive grassy pathway. Continue along this bridleway, passing a small copse to your right, and ponds to your left: coots may be seen on these ponds. The ground may be muddy here after rains. Pass over a rickety wooden plank bridge. The Old Mill can be spied to your right over the fields. When you reach a footpath junction turn right, and ignore the footpath to the left a few hundred yards further on. You will emerge into Mill Lane.

8. Turn left into Mill Lane, and follow it as it bears gently downhill and rightwards, leading you back to the village of Willaston. The Nags Head, the first pub you reach in Willaston, was boasting the Whitbread Cask Collection at the time of the authors' visit and may be worth a diversion. Turn right to

find yourself back at the village green; the Pollard Inn is tucked away behind the green.

The Pollard Inn

29. NESTON

Route: Neston – Ness – Little Neston – Neston

Distance: 7 miles

Map: OS Pathfinder 756 (1:25000) Ellesmere Port (West)

Start: Neston Railway Station (SJ293777)

Access: Train from Bidston and Wrexham; details from British Rail on 051 709 9696. Road access from Chester and Liverpool on the A540. There is ample parking space in Neston, including car parks close to the railway station. For details of bus services to Neston, contact Cheshire Bus on Chester 602666.

The Wheatsheaf, Ness (051 336 2150)

The Wheatsheaf has a large pleasant bar, comfortably furnished, offering Thwaites Mild and Bitter and Craftsmans Traditional Premium Bitter. It is open all day Monday to Saturday (11.00 am to 11.00 pm); normal Sunday hours. Food is available every lunchtime, until 2.30 pm Monday to Friday, and until 2.00 pm on Saturday and Sunday. There is a children's play area outside and some tables overlooking the Dee estuary. Families are welcomed. When the authors visited, a seat outside in the sun and a pint of mild were very welcome. Lady Hamilton used to reside at Swan Cottage, opposite the Wheatsheaf, although it is not recorded whether she visited the hostelry for a pint of Thwaites, or indeed whether Nelson ever popped in for a pie and pint!

The Harp, Little Neston (051 336 6980)

The Harp is a beautiful whitewashed building on what used to be the banks of the Dee, now the marshes stretch away in front of it and the water is remote. The pub has two small, cosy bars with comfortably padded seating. Real ales on offer when we visited included Whitbread Trophy, Weetwood and Timothy Taylor's Landlord. The staff look after the beer well: the Taylor's Landlord was gorgeous on our visit. There are tables outside with lovely views across the estuary, and a beer garden to the rear. This a very peaceful place, as the only cars are those of visitors to the pub.

Neston

Neston's early prosperity, like that of Parkgate, depended upon the River Dee and its progressive silting. Neston's quay was built in the 16th century as a response to the decline of the port of Chester due to silting; Neston was to be superseded by Parkgate in the 19th century for the same reason. Once the silting of the Dee removed the immediate connection between Neston and the Dee, a relative decline was suffered, only reversed by the construction of the Hooton – Parkgate Railway in the mid 19th century. The railway attracted new residents; it also carried coal from the Ness Mine. This rail line closed in 1962, and its route now forms part of the Wirral Way. Neston retains rail links to Wrexham and Bidston. Neston is now a pleasant small town, retaining a sea air.

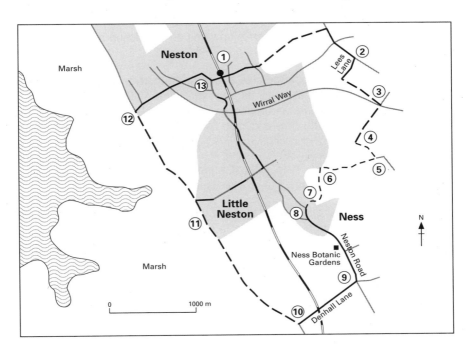

The Walk

1. From the railway station turn left into Raby Road and continue as it changes its name to Blackeys Lane. When the lane curves to the left carry straight on along the footpath signed to Chester High Road. This is a wide lane at first, narrowing to a path with pasture on each side. The path is enclosed by a hedge and a fence and continues through farmland, past ponds and woodland. At the end of the path turn right onto the A540 – although this is a busy road, there is a footway and you will leave it soon – carry on past the Shrewsbury Arms.

2. Take a right-hand turn down Lees Lane signed to Little Neston. The lane takes you past farm buildings on the right, then take a footpath to the left, marked with a horseshoe sign. The path which can be muddy, as horses' hooves churn the way, is surrounded by trees and fields.

3. After a while you will see a path off to the right leading up a steep embankment: this is our route. Climb up the embankment and across the Wirral Way, and pass down the steps on the other side, signed "Cuckoo Lane to Little Neston". Cross the stile and turn right into the lane, continue as it becomes a path sloping gently upwards and enclosed on both sides by hedgerows.

4. At the top of the hill cross the stile and take the path to your left. Keep the hedge to your right as you walk through the field. Although the elevation is only 60 metres the views all around are extensive. Cross another stile and continue along the path now enclosed by a hedge to the right and a fence to the left.

5. Turn right along a wide path, almost a lane really. Note Windle Hill Nature Reserve to the right on the site of a disused rubbish tip.

6. The path emerges into Woodfall Lane. Turn left just before the school buildings, along the right-hand side of a small children's play area. Cross the stile at the end of the play area and take the path across the field, almost straight ahead from the stile.

7. At the corner of the field, cross a stile to your right and continue towards a row of cottages. Pass over or through another stile and down the steps, to

follow the path at the bottom of the cottage gardens. Carry straight on down towards the road, turn left out of Combers Lane onto the main road.

A welcome break at The Wheatsheaf

8. Almost immediately The Wheatsheaf becomes visible on the right, time to stop for a welcome rest and possibly a pint of Thwaites. On leaving the pub continue along the road which soon leads you past Ness Botanic gardens, part of Liverpool University: if you relish a diversion, the gardens are open to the public.

9. Beyond the gardens, turn right down Denhall Lane, past a turning circle for buses. A lovely view down to and across the Dee opens up now, there is a well sited bench here. Follow the lane down towards the river, this is an attractive lane enclosed by hedgerows, which takes you across the railway.

10. At the bottom of the road turn right along a footpath signed "Quayside 1 mile" The marshes are home to sheep and bird life. The path is wide and tarmac. Continue past Denhall House Farm, which has an impressive weather vane on the roof. The path goes through a strange sequence of

surfaces, tarmac to broken cockle shells to bricks to mud to grass as you progress further. The path eventually becomes part of the marshes on the final stretch, and you join the sheep briefly. A fenced-off section appears in front of you, the path bears to the right and upwards, and then turns left along a lane with houses on each side. The view soon opens out again across the marshes.

11. The Harp Inn soon appears to the right: time for a welcome halt and refreshment. On leaving the pub it is possible to continue along the path, then take the road on the right, turning left onto Burton Road and back to the railway station. However, a more attractive option is to continue along the coastal path. This is a well-walked traditional route, though not a formal right of way. Continue along the path across a stile into a field and along the path parallel to the river bank. This path leads you to stepping stones across a small stream. The old stones on the bank show the remains of the old quayside. This once served a local coal mine; it is now hard to believe industry ever touched this area. The quay first became active in the 16th century, when silting of the River Dee made access to Chester impossible for ships. However, the River soon retreated further and ships anchored at Parkgate. By the early 18th century the quay was disused. Cross another stile and follow a narrow paved path, the grasses to your left are tall and impressive. Wooden bridges carry you across narrow water channels.

12. As you reach a row of houses ahead, turn right, away from the river, down a path bounded by the fences of the gardens and fields. Carry on down the road ahead, Moorside Lane, and a bridge takes you across the Wirral Way. At the junction, with Parkgate and Neston United Reformed Church to your left, go straight on up Buggen Lane. The lane has attractive red sandstone garden walls.

13. At the end of the lane turn right down Park Street past the telephone exchange on the junction. At the next junction go straight down Raby Road which bears left to the railway station and the end of the walk.

30. HELSBY

Route: Helsby – Helsby Marshes – Helsby Hill – Helsby

Distance: 5.5 miles

Map: OS Pathfinder 757 (1:25000) Ellesmere Port (East)

Start: Helsby Railway Station (SJ487757)

Access: Helsby lies 1.5 miles east of Junction 14 on the M56. Access is via the A56 Chester Road. Car Parking is available in the station car park.

Helsby is connected to Liverpool and Birkenhead by a frequent rail service. Helsby also enjoys a train service to Manchester, Warrington and North Wales.

Railway Inn, Chester Road, Helsby (0928 724386)

The Railway Inn is a pleasant public house serving the full range of Greenalls real ales. There is a double-L shaped bar in the centre of attractive corridor-style bars and lounges. Lunches and evening meals are available every day, and there is a garden and outdoor play area. The Railway opens all day Friday and Saturday (11.00 am – 11.00 pm); between 11.00 am & 3.00 pm and 5.30 & 11.00 pm Monday to Thursday; normal Sunday hours apply.

Helsby

Helsby is a linear village along the Chester Road (A56), much quieter in terms of traffic since the construction of the M56, but still noisy as the roar of the motorway can be heard at most times. Helsby Hill overlooks the town; it stands at 141 metres and is owned by the National Trust. The red Cheshire sandstone quarried from Helsby Hill has been used to build the Anglican cathedrals in both Liverpool and Chester.

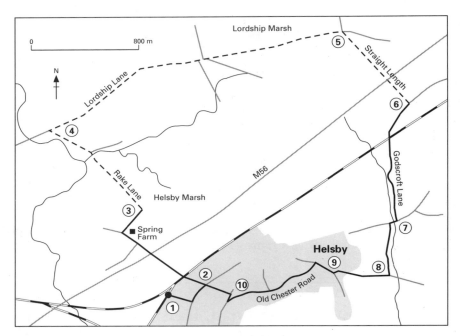

The Walk

1. From Helsby Station walk up Station Drive and turn left along Chester Road opposite the Coffee Shop.

2. Turn left just in front of the Railway Inn and walk down Lower Rake Lane, crossing in turn the railway line and the M56. The lane may be muddy here as cows from the nearby farms use the same bridge to cross the motorway. Pass Spring Farm, and bear right with the road, keeping the ditch to your right.

3. Take the first turning on the left down Rake Lane, before you reach Hill View Farm on the right. Note the Poacherwatch sign which has been erected here by the Cheshire Constabulary. There is a curious combination here of rural animal grazing, Mersey industry to the left and to the right at Runcorn, and the M56 roaring behind you. Continue to make for the large bank (levee) ahead of you, keeping the industry to your left.

4. Turn right at the end of the lane, just before the bank, into Lordship Lane. The banked area to your left, and others which you will see, are quaintly termed "canal deposit dumps"; they are the tipping sites for residue from the Manchester Ship Canal. Admire the fine views to your right to Helsby Hill, and further ahead to Beacon Hill at Frodsham. You will find the path truly deserted here: your only companions will be bunnies and birdies. Continue straight ahead at the end of the bank along Lordship Lane, and keep Lordship Marsh to your left.

5. At the lane junction, take the lane to the right, the wonderfully named "Straight Length", and head towards the bridge over the M56 (note: *not* the bridge seen to the left). Cross over the motorway and walk on to the end of the lane.

6. Turn right into Godscroft Lane, and walk towards the Chester Road, passing under a railway bridge and passing Godscroft Hall to your left.

7. At Chester Road, turn right, cross over, and turn left down the little lane, immediately before the Helsby name sign. Keep the small stream to your left.

8. By the wooden footbridge, turn right up the concrete steps, pass over a stile, and follow the footpath over the fields towards a telegraph pole. Pass over the next stile, and take the narrow twitchell straight on. Cross over the next stile, and pass over the field. Climb over the broken stile at the right-hand edge of the field, and pass along another very narrow pathway.

9. At the end of the path, pass through the gate and turn right along Bates Lane. Turn left at the next junction along Old Chester Road. Admire the fine red Cheshire sandstone of Helsby Hill all around you. If you wish to ascend to the summit of Helsby Hill, several public footpaths are signed off to the left. Keep on with the road, and begin to descend.

10. When you reach a road on your right called The Heights, turn down this road and bear with it as it turns leftwards and goes gently downhill. At the bottom of the road, you will find yourself back at the Chester Road. The Railway Inn lies opposite, where you can quench your thirst. The railway station and car park lies just along the Chester Road to your left.

Helsby Railway Station

Explore the countryside with Sigma!

We have a wide selection of guides to individual towns, plus outdoor activities centred on walking and cycling in the great outdoors throughout England and Wales. This is a recent selection:

Cycling . . .

CYCLE UK! The definitive guide to leisure cycling
– Les Lumsdon *(£9.95)*

OFF-BEAT CYCLING & MOUNTAIN BIKING IN THE PEAK DISTRICT
– Clive Smith *(£6.95)*

MORE OFF-BEAT CYCLING IN THE PEAK DISTRICT
– Clive Smith *(£6.95)*

50 BEST CYCLE RIDES IN CHESHIRE
– edited by Graham Beech *(£7.95)*

CYCLING IN THE COTSWOLDS
– Stephen Hill *(£6.95)*

CYCLING IN THE LAKE DISTRICT
– John Wood *(£7.95)*

CYCLING IN SOUTH WALES
– Rosemary Evans *(£7.95)*

CYCLING IN NORTH STAFFORDSHIRE
– Linda Wain *(£7.95)*

BY-WAY TRAVELS SOUTH OF LONDON
– Geoff Marshall *(£7.95)*

Walking . . .

RAMBLES IN NORTH WALES
– Roger Redfern

HERITAGE WALKS IN THE PEAK DISTRICT
– Clive Price

EAST CHESHIRE WALKS
– Graham Beech

WEST CHESHIRE WALKS
– Jen Darling

WEST PENNINE WALKS
– Mike Cresswell

NEWARK AND SHERWOOD RAMBLES
– Malcolm McKenzie

RAMBLES AROUND NOTTINGHAM & DERBY
– Keith Taylor

RAMBLES AROUND MANCHESTER
– Mike Cresswell

WESTERN LAKELAND RAMBLES
– Gordon Brown

WELSH WALKS:
Dolgellau and the Cambrian Coast
– Laurence Main and Morag Perrott

WELSH WALKS:
Aberystwyth and District
– Laurence Main and Morag Perrott

– all of these books are currently £6.95 each.

Long-distance walking . . .

THE GREATER MANCHESTER BOUNDARY WALK – Graham Phythian

THE THIRLMERE WAY – Tim Cappelli

THE FURNESS TRAIL – Tim Cappelli

THE MARCHES WAY – Les Lumsdon

– all £6.95 each

We also publish:

A fabulous series of 'Pub Walks' books for just about every popular walking area in the UK, all featuring access by public transport

A new series of investigations into the Supernatural,
Myth and Magic

Superb illustrated books on Manchester's football teams

– plus many more entertaing and educational books being regularly added to our list. All of our books are available from your local bookshop. In case of difficulty, or to obtain our complete catalogue, please contact:

Sigma Leisure, 1 South Oak Lane, Wilmslow, Cheshire SK9 6AR

Phone: 0625 – 531035   Fax: 0625 – 536800

ACCESS and VISA orders welcome – call our friendly sales staff or use our 24 hour Answerphone service! Most orders are despatched on the day we receive your order – you could be enjoying our books in just a couple of days.